AF574745

By the same author

Discovering the Isle of Wight

Fiction

A Far Cry from Clammergoose
High Walk to Wandlemere
Ravens in Winter

OTHER BOOKS IN THE VILLAGE SERIES

Avon Villages
Edmund J. Mason and Dorrien Mason
Cornish Villages
Donald R. Rawe
Cotswold Villages
June R. Lewis
Cumbrian Villages
Kenneth Smith
Devon Villages
S. H. Burton
Dorset Villages
Roland Gant
Durham Villages
Harry Thompson
Highland Villages
James Shaw Grant
Kent Villages
Alan Bignell
Lancashire Villages
Jessica Lofthouse
Lowland Scottish Villages
Maurice Lindsay
Norfolk Villages
David H. Kennett
Northumberland Villages
Godfrey Watson
Shropshire and Herefordshire Villages
George H. Haines
Suffolk Villages
Allan Jobson
Surrey Villages
Derek Pitt and Michael Shaw
Sussex Villages
Michael H. C. Baker
Yorkshire Villages
G. Bernard Wood

Isle of Wight Villages

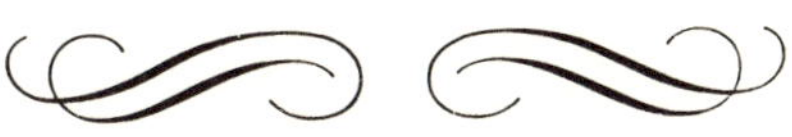

PATRICIA SIBLEY

PHOTOGRAPHS BY
JO COOKSON

ROBERT HALE · LONDON

© 1983 by Patricia Sibley
First published in Great Britain 1983

ISBN 0 7090 0833 3

Robert Hale Limited
Clerkenwell House
Clerkenwell Green
London EC1R 0HT

Photoset in Palatino by
Kelly Typesetting Limited
Bradford-on-Avon, Wiltshire
and printed in Great Britain by
Redwood Burn Limited, Trowbridge, Wilts
Bound by WBC Bookbinders Limited

Contents

Illustrations

Between pages 32 and 33

Between pages 80 and 81

Between pages 128 and 129

Between pages 176 and 177

Acknowledgments

My grateful thanks to the many people who helped provide material for this book. These include:

Sheila White for permission to quote from her book *Twelve Hundred Years in St. Helens.*

The Isle of Wight County Record Office for general assistance and permission to use the Memoirs of Mr F. O'B. Adams of Bembridge.

Mr S. Matthews for permission to quote from his *Memoirs of Seaview.*

The Maritime Museum, Bembridge.

Mr Peter Adams of Flamingo Park.

The Editor of the *Isle of Wight County Press* for permission to quote extracts from his paper.

Mr Raymond Young of Haseley Manor.

Messrs Fleming of Robin Hill Country Park, and Mr L. R. Fennelly for showing me his excavations of the Roman villa there.

Mr J Trzebski of Morton Manor.

Mrs M. Munday-Whitaker of the Lilliput Dolls' Museum, Brading.

Mr Cephas Howard of Arreton Craft Centre.

Mrs Beatrice Coffin for her memoirs of Whippingham and Folly Inn.

Mr Ted Gustar for his memories of Northwood and Marks Corner.

Mrs Roma Warne for her memories of Gurnard.

Mr Anthony Goddard of Barton Manor.

Miss W. Chappell for information on the R.S.P.C.A. Animal Home, Bohemia Corner.

Mr and Mrs C. Wadsworth of Rookley Country Park.

Mr and Mrs C. Pearce of Park View, Wroxall.

Mrs L. Vanassche of Lake Farm Riding Centre, Rookley.

Mr O. Morris of Newbridge, for his memories of Niton.

Mrs Teddy Flint of The Bird Hospital, St Lawrence.

Mrs Joan Wolfendon of Peacock Vane, Bonchurch.

Mr Simon Dabell, of Blackgang Chine.

Mr David Tomalin, County Archaeological Officer.

Mr Robert Taylor of Hill Farm, Gatcombe, for information on that village.

Mr Norton Green for information on Gatcombe.

Dr Jack Jones, Curator of Carisbrooke Castle, and Mr Ray Jones for information on the castle flora.

Mrs J. McGougan of The Hermitage, Chale.

John and Sheila Francis of Chessel Pottery.

Mr Alec Downer for his memories of Calbourne.

Pat Ewbank, Warden of Newtown Nature Reserve.

Mr Marks of the Hunt Kennels, Gatcombe

County Federation of Women's Institutes for permission to use scrapbook material.

Richard Hutchings for information on Shorwell.

Mr Moorman Twyman for his memories of Freshwater.

Miss Gertie Turner for her memories of Totland.

Mrs E. Satherley for permission to use *The Making of Bricks*, by Francis Pritchett.

Mrs Gladys Harrison for permission to quote from correspondence.

Mrs H. Chappell for permission to use *Annals of Bembridge Lifeboats*, by R. Watson.

Mrs D. G. Wilson for permission to use her booklet on Fernhill.

Mr C. Bawden for permission to use his *History of Newchurch*.

Mr Roy Fallick for the use of his grandfather's memoirs as gamekeeper at Swainston.

Mr R. F. Sprake for permission to use his booklet on Shalfleet.

Mr J. Kenneth Major for background information from his *Mills of the Isle of Wight*.

Dr Christopher Young, Inspector of Ancient Monuments for the Department of the Environment, for permission to report on his excavations at Carisbrooke Castle.

Anne Marks for typing the manuscript.

Note:
Asterisks in the main text denote that more information will be found in my earlier book *Discovering the Isle of Wight* (Robert Hale, 1977).

0
Miles
5
0
km
5
Lymington
T
H
E
Hamstead
Porchfie
Park
hurs
Fore
Newtown
Hurst
Castle
Yarmouth
Thorley
Shalfleet
A3054
B3403
Wellow
Newbridge
B3401
Freshwater
West Yar
Totland
B3399
Calbourne
Freshwater Bay
The
Needles
B3322
B3323
Hulverstone
Brooke
Mottistone
Shorwell
Brighstone
A3055

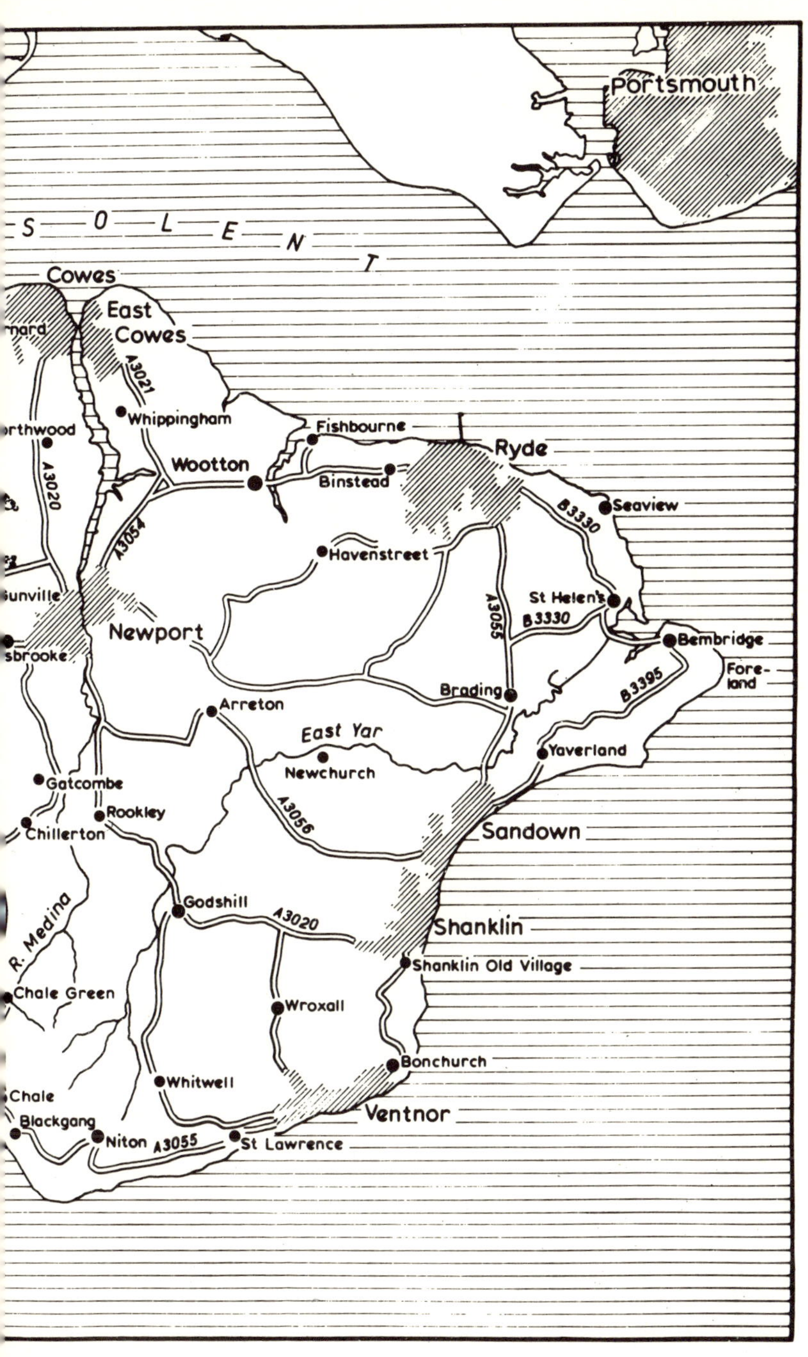
Portsmouth
S O L E N T
Cowes
East Cowes
A3021
Whippingham
Wootton
Fishbourne
Ryde
Binstead
Seaview
B3330
A3020
A3054
Havenstreet
St Helen's
A3055
B3330
Newport
Bembridge
Fore-land
B3395
Brading
Arreton
East Yar
Newchurch
Yaverland
Gatcombe
Rookley
Chillerton
A3056
Sandown
R. Medina
Godshill
A3020
Shanklin
Shanklin Old Village
Chale Green
Wroxall
Bonchurch
Whitwell
Chale
Ventnor
Blackgang
Niton
A3055
St Lawrence

Preface

On the south, great cliffs fall sheer to the foam of the Channel; on the north the island spreads away, diamond shaped, to a gleaming ribbon, the sheltered, narrow waters of the Solent. From St Catherine's Down, nearly eight hundred feet above the most southerly point, the land falls away to a wide undulating plain, the Lower Greensand, a patchwork of plough and meadow with here and there a cluster of roofs round a church tower, white gulls following a red tractor.

Beyond, a line of chalk downs, grey-green and bare, rears up against the sky, crossing the island from utmost east to west—where they meet the sea plunging in spectacular white cliffs at the Needles and Culver. Only in central Wight is there a gap through which flows the River Medina, and its long valley gives a glimpse of the flat Oligocene or clay lands of northern Wight.

From this height, the land seems idyllic, unchanged even for hundreds of years, yet it has seen invasions by Romans and

Saxons, raids by French and Dane, the rise and fall of a great monastery, threat of invasion by Spain, France and Germany, enclosing of land and rise of smuggling, a new fashion for seaside holidays, the residence of Queen Victoria and a tidal wave of twentieth-century building.

The one abiding influence is that gleam of water which looks from here so narrow—the Solent. It cuts off trade, giving the island a higher than average rate of unemployment, keeps the cost of living high, cuts off the island from the mainstream of cultural events, isolates families from mainland relations. Young people go away to train for careers and many never return.

Isolation may seem too strong a word—to those not living here. Of course there are ferries, and the hydrofoil takes only seven minutes, but they are expensive, seldom operate late in the evening: the fuss of parking the car, catching a ferry and arranging connections on the mainland puts up a psychological, as well as financial, barrier which will only be truly understood by other island dwellers.

So why do more and more people come to retire here, giving the island a bias of elderly residents? And why are islanders up in arms at the latest of many schemes to connect island to mainland?

Because Wight *is* an island, the pace of life is slower: there are no motorways, noisy airports or city traffic: in spite of all the new building it is still a beautiful place to live in—and island rats do not race, they tend to amble round rick-yards.

Floods of summer visitors and a smaller flow of new residents prevent the island growing too inward looking, but its comparative isolation has thrown the people very much on their own resources. It *is* possible to see a matinée at a London theatre and catch the last ferry, but it is an exhausting and expensive day, so the island boasts many flourishing dramatic societies, likewise choirs and craft guilds, morris men, bird watchers, steam train fanatics—there is an extraordinarily rich variety of things going on. Only visitors ask, "What do you do in the winter?" for September, when the tourists depart, is when the pace of life begins to quicken in town and village alike.

The eastern end, the nearest to a big city and en route to London is perhaps the most influenced by the mainland. Move westward and Wight becomes steadily less sophisticated, more itself, so this book follows that pattern, starting with the eastern peninsula, moving westward along roads or river valleys.

Creek and copse, windy down and sheltered harbour, wild cliffs and hanging woods, the lush palm-growing Undercliff, cows in a field, forest and secret stream—all these go to make up the Isle of Wight, a lovely and varied countryside to suit every mood, with hundreds of miles of footpaths and villages of incomparable variety, only to be explored truly on foot, at an ambling pace.

1

The Eastern Peninsula

At the eastern end of the Isle of Wight, cliffs heave up into the great green bulk of Culver Down, then slope away to wide marshy meadows and the shining waters of Bembridge Harbour, now almost land-locked. On the wooded slope beyond lies St Helens, and round Node's Point to the north, Seaview.

A map dated 1810 shows only a few isolated farms here, with hamlets of fishermen's cottages along the coast; the farm names included Well Parrocke, Ghosts, Oatens, Marepool and Chough Shore. So Bembridge is not really old as a village, but occupies a site rich in history. Once it was almost an island, for the harbour stretched right up to Brading, while the low land between Brading and Sandown was often flooded. When the first bridge was built over the River Yar in the fourteenth century, the seaward portion was called Within Bridge, which over the years shortened to Binbrydge, and finally Bembridge.

Some of the early settlers were the people of the Bronze Age who have left their burial mounds, or tumuli, up on the downs. A harbour stretching miles inland tempted foreign invaders, Romans, Saxons and Danes. In A.D. 897 King Alfred's navy fought the Vikings' ships off Foreland. The first historical settlement seems to have been under Culver Down, where tradition describes a town called Woolverton which was destroyed in a fourteenth-century raid by the French. While many tales of Woolverton are legendary, there is documentary proof that a chapel stood here in 1305, founded by the ancestors of John Gyberd, who paid the monks of Quarr Abbey to say Mass each week. In the nineteenth century and since, some medieval tiles and pottery have been found in St Urian's Copse, which now covers the site.

Several French raids culminated in the attack of 1545 when a large French fleet was sighted rounding Bembridge Point. The King himself was camped on Southsea Common, and the British fleet ready at Portsmouth. To tempt it into battle, the French landed and began to advance along the lower slopes of Culver Down, but were so violently attacked by the "Home Guard" of that period, that the survivors retreated in haste, never to return.

So the lands round the harbour were left in peace, to become small agricultural and fishing communities. At this time the harbour mouth was further north, so that the spit of land now known as St Helen's Duver was then attached to the Bembridge side, where tenants of the Worsley estate held grazing rights. Within the harbour flourished an oyster fishery. In 1759 Mary Oglander wrote to her husband at nearby Nunwell, "I beg if the oysters are good you will have some pickled, and send one little barrel to my grandmother for she cannot dispense with many."

Foreland is the most easterly point of the island, blunt and undramatic with small yellow-brown cliffs perpetually slipping away, forming green ledges patched with willows and ponds. Once it was a fishing hamlet, those willows the descendants of withy beds grown for the making of lobster pots. Weighting them down with stones was called "steening" the pots; the fishermen also made large ones called penning pots, which were sunk in a pool to keep bait alive. Local boys would often make catches at low tide by going out on the reef, tipping up loose rocks with a piece of wood and grabbing the tenant lobster by the tail.

By the eighteenth century, smuggling went hand in hand, or boat in boat, with fishing, and the Crab and Lobster Inn, a little cottage pub at Foreland, was one of its headquarters. "Fishing trips" often brought back catches of spirits, tobacco or French lace, the copse at Lane End and a cave in Culver Cliff being two of their hiding places. The revenue authorities built watch houses at the Point and near Foreland, but how could they fight a witch? Molly Downer lived alone in Hill Way, shunned by the villagers who called her a witch, her only friend, the vicar—and presumably her fellow smugglers. According to J. Brummell's ballad:

Her guiles she used with every ruse
To bring in free trade brandy booze.
The customs men, so runs the tale
Would at her name turn deathly pale.

When she died in 1835, the vicar was much embarrassed to find himself her sole legatee, and had the cottage burned to the ground.

The Napoleonic Wars had cast a fear of invasion over the island once again and nowhere was more vulnerable than the harbour, so watch houses were manned and plans laid for a new fort on Bembridge Down. A field was leased to make the bricks at a monthly rate of two shillings per thousand.

But as in West Wight, it was the peaceful invasion of visitors which altered the face of Bembridge for ever and turned it into a fashionable resort. First, a new road from Brading opened up the peninsula, then a steamer service began operating from a pier near the Point to the mainland. For hundreds of years the few inhabitants of the Isle of Bembridge had had to row across the harbour mouth if they wished to worship at the nearest church, St Helen's, but with the growth of population it was decided to build a church in the centre of the village. Sited over "blue slipper" clay, this fell down and another with stronger foundations was built there in 1847.

Holy Trinity is a spacious, light church in Early English style with much bright Victorian stained glass and some striking wall tablets, one of which depicts St George in mosaic. Just outside is a newer memorial, a plain gravestone carved with an aeroplane to mark the grave of John Britten, co-founder of Britten-Norman, the local firm famous for the design and building of the Islander and Trislander series of planes.

But to return to the nineteenth century. By 1879 the steamer *Blanche* called twice a day, bringing visitors from Portsmouth and Southsea. After many attempts down the centuries, the upper reaches of the harbour were at last reclaimed when the present embankment was finished for the railway. Bembridge station opening in 1882. (As it was the terminus, a team of men had to manhandle the engine round on a turntable.) One can judge the prosperity of the new tourist trade by the vast size of the Royal Spithead Hotel opened opposite the station at this time.

A guide of the period said: "The picturesque village of Bembridge has become one of the most favourite resorts in the island, so beautiful is its position, so healthy its breezy air and so noble its scenic effects. In the vicinity are several genteel residences, picturesquely situated among leaf and shade."

Side by side with the tourist boom, other enterprises were at work. Early in the century a William Wallis sailed his cutter *Amity* southward from England, landed at Foreland and set up as a pilot, by no means a peaceful profession at that time, work being fiercely competitive—whoever reached a ship first would get the job of bringing her in or out of Spithead. If a cutter, having beaten its rivals and delivered a pilot, found itself near the Dorset coast, it would bring back a cargo of Portland stone so as not to waste the journey.

Another important event in village life was the stationing of the first lifeboat, at Lane End.

Bembridge Ledge, those same rocks famous for crabs and lobsters, stretches a mile and a half out to sea and has wrecked many a ship seeking shelter in St Helen's Roads. In 1867, a Norwegian boat, *Egbert*, loaded with barley, ran aground on the ledge in a storm and began to break up: in an effort to climb above the surging waves, the crew took to the rigging, the usual procedure. When the wreck was sighted by a fisherman, an urgent summons was sent round the village and a volunteer crew of fishermen set off in an open boat in the teeth of an easterly gale. When they managed to reach the *Egbert*, a small boy was too frightened to let go the rigging and had to be carried down into the small boat, but all the crew were rescued.

This splendid act of bravery inspired the people of Worcester to subscribe money for a lifeboat and so the first lifeboat station was set up in Bembridge to house *The City of Worcester*. At Lane End, the old lifeboat house is now used for the small inshore rescue boat and a long concrete pier, built in 1922, leads out to the present boathouse, which is sometimes open to the public. One of the steamers plying from the mainland, the *Bembridge*, carried a permanent passenger, a dog called Sir Henry Squash who collected for the Royal National Lifeboat Institution and was rewarded each day with half a pint of beer.

In 1873 this stylish resort was threatened with industrial development. High seas in Whitecliff Bay uncovered a seam of coal. Letters full of excitement at the find flew to and fro. "It extends from cliffs to low water mark, a distance of seventy yards and on out to sea . . . it burns well." Later a twenty-foot shaft was sunk and a further letter proclaimed, "Whitecliff Bay is likely to become a place of some importance from the fact of large deposits of coal."

Fortunately perhaps, such hopes came to nothing. An old dredger called *Fanny Grab* fought a continual battle to keep a deep-water channel open, for by this time coal was brought directly into the harbour by the steam colliers *Allerwash* and *Ellington* and distributed by the "puffer", the little steam train which shunted between Bembridge and Brading. Near the station stood the Pilot Boat Inn, the Marine Hotel and the Prince of Wales public house. A few minutes before the train was due to leave, a porter would ring a loud hand bell and engine driver and crew would emerge from one or other pub. Side by side with the new transport stood a stables and a blacksmith's shop where the farrier wore the traditional smith's apron, a whole sheepskin.

So by the turn of the century many large summer residences had been built for "overners", that is, people living on the mainland, and the fishing hamlets transformed by this invasion of more sophisticated society. Nevertheless the youth of the village still congregated in Lacey's Field, their headquarters being the gate. The farmer tarred it, then hammered in spikes, but still they leaned and yarned, displaying the peculiar island genius for nicknames. Here met Ratty, Mutton, Bottleass and Didler, while all Roberts were known as Breezer. And they still used powerfully descriptive old island phrases such as lop-lolly, meaning a bit simple, or duck bottom high to a goose—rather short. "Er looks a tuppenny hambone in that ol' donkey's breakfast'' meant she was overdressed in that straw hat!

Today Bembridge is a widely scattered sprawl, much of it modern, like the road down to Foreland where summer huts and a car park stand among the descendants of withy beds. There is a High Street and clumps of shops further out too, but various large houses with spacious grounds and mature trees still lend it a pleasant rural air, from the lower slopes of Culver, right down to the harbour.

The Maritime Museum, established on the site of a bakery in 1978, will do much to enrich a visit to Bembridge. Among its treasures are many elegant ship models, photographs of the lifeboat being manhandled into the sea and also of the harbour before it was drained, the story of the Nab Lighthouse, and even a mermaid! One of the best exhibits is a large model of Brading Haven clearly showing the whole history of its reclamation from the fourteenth century onward.

Bembridge is a splendid walking centre. A walk round the harbour might well start at the Pilot Boat, a pub built to look like a ship ashore with decks and portholes; even the menu is nautical—gammon and pineapple is called Ark Royal. Close by stands the Row Barge with a picturesque sign board, while the enormous building once the Spithead Hotel is now a college. Along the harbour wall various houseboats are permanently moored while beyond them there is always a coming and going of small craft, the most striking being Bembridge Redwings, whose club was founded in 1896.

A walk across the old harbour starts at the windmill, opened in summer by the National Trust. Out on the airfield beyond lie the latest products of the firm now called Pilatus Britten-Norman, and underfoot an old stone dyke, part of the original harbour known locally as Duggers Wall. Well-signposted paths lead on past St Urian's Copse to Brading, or across the road and up the steep slopes of Culver Down, surmounted by a cross to the Earl of Yarborough, raised in 1849 and amazingly expensive at £2,900. This included £104 for horse keep, and hire of horse for 763 days, £114. The wide and lovely view extends from St Boniface Down in the south right round green eastern Wight to the little wooded cliffs by St Helens and across to the mainland. The stately prose of a Victorian guide describes "the chalky precipices of Culver

Cliff, about five hundred feet in height and perpendicular, at whose base roar the loud billows of the ocean, sending up a misty, foamy spray that on a sunny morn rolls about these precipitous cliffs like clouds of resplendent glory". Herring gulls nest here, while unusual flowers of the chalk include early gentian and dwarf mouse ear.

Nestled beneath the landward flank of Culver stood the village of Yaverland, the name originally said to be derived from Evreland, land of the boars, then corrupted to overland. When Legh Richmond, later famous as author of *The Dairyman's Daughter*, was minister here, he described Yaverland as he saw it about 1800. "One road ascends between several rural cottages from the seashore which adjoins the lower part of the village street, another winds round the side of the adjacent hill and a third leads to the church by a gently rising approach between high banks covered with young trees, bushes, ivy, hedge plants and wild flowers."

Today, with the encroachment of Sandown and the disappearance of old cottages, there is little sense of village, but the heart of it, manor house and church remain in a peaceful setting of woods and pasture.

The Norman family of de Aula built the original manor house and the cottages grew up round it to house retainers, but "all ye winter they could not come to Brading Church except they went about by Sandam two myles", so the de Aulas built a chapel too.

Various folk tales of this Culver country centre round a wicked pedlar who lived in a cave, and his enemy, the Holy Man, possibly a monk, called John. One day a fisherman was lamenting to the pedlar that his maid hardly seemed to love him any more. The pedlar said that was because she was in love with the knight of Yaverland and had come to despise a mere fisherman, "So why don't you go out the next dark of the moon," he suggested, "and set a rush light to the manor thatch?"

The fisherman thought this a splendid idea and later set off, but was met by the Holy Man and dissuaded from his fell deed and so Yaverland was saved.

The present beautiful stone manor house, on its knoll behind the church, was built about 1620 and is still a private residence, but the chapel below is open winter and summer. Built in the twelfth century, it has two finely carved late Norman arches.

Over the entrance one is set a stone head, locally known as The Monk. Could this be the Holy Man John? If so, he wears a peculiarly sardonic grin.

Preserved on a bracket stands a huge cauldron-shaped earthenware cooking pot, found in a wall during the Victorian restoration. It is thought to have been used by the masons who built the original church in the twelfth century.

On the walls, several tablets remind one that this was for hundreds of years a garrison church, for troops stationed in the various forts built along this coast from Henry VIII's reign onward. During the last war the Yaverland boundary with Sandown was one of the outfalls of PLUTO (Pipe Line under the Ocean), which took fuel across to the invasion beaches of Normandy.

Behind Yaverland the high white cliffs of Culver slope down to a dramatic change of colour at Redcliff Bay, where the Wealden clay has yielded many dinosaur remains, including the skull of one now known as Yaverlandia: fossils of turtleshell, megalosaurus and tree fern have been found here also and all may be seen in the nearby Museum of Geology in Sandown.

The older generation of islanders still use traditional forms of direction. From the coast you always go *in* to Newport. In Bembridge usage "down top o'shore" meant overlooking the beach. You went *up* Brading, but *down* Sandown, *down* harbour but *up* harbour gardens. And you could go "over S'nel'ns" by the little ferry across the harbour mouth, which still runs in summer.

This lands on the point of a vast sandy spit called the Duver with rows of beach huts—old railway carriages in fact. The shore is rich in shells and popular with bathers, though it is doubtful if they give a thought to the by-law passed a hundred years ago. "No person above the age of twelve shall—while bathing—knowingly or willingly approach within fifty yards of a bather of the other sex."

A sea wall leads along to a curious slice of whitewashed tower, which is where the history of St Helens really begins. In fulfilment of a vow, the Saxon invader Cadwalla gave one quarter of the Isle of Wight to Bishop Wilfred of Chichester. "Wylfryde was ye fyrst in these parts that taught men to catch fish, both with hookes and nettes." He also sent his chaplain to St Helens to build a church. In those days it would have been a wooden building and was almost certainly burned down in tenth-century raids by the pillaging Danes. But the next invaders, the Normans, were great builders and founded a priory here on the shore, attached to the Cluniac Priory in Much Wenlock.

At that time the village was known as Hertham, though part was known as Eddington, a name which survives in Eddington Road. The splendid Norman name Beaurepayr is retained by the farm now called Beaper. Soon the Priory estate included a pigeon house, warren, quarries and a mill, but in 1414 all religious houses linked with alien foundations—in this case Cluny—were dissolved. St Helens Priory was closed and its lands eventually given to Eton College, though the church was left for village use.

For a long time there is no record of a priest, and soon the church had fallen into decay. An account of the parish in 1648 says, "You know well the situation of the church, at every high water now of late years washed by the sea . . . the crash of the sea in foule weather hath borne down all or part of the church walls, raysed stones as big as the strength of men were able to move, and the whole church, since the taking in of the haven, not a little endangered." At one time horses were stabled inside the walls. When a parson was appointed, he spent his time in "continued haunting of ale houses in Brading", so that Sir John Oglander, chronicler of these parts was forced to observe, "the church hath been evil served and worse repaired". Finally in 1656, Commissioners sent by Oliver Cromwell recommended that "The church be taken down 'ere it fall and set up in the midst of the parish." In fact the new church was not built for another sixty-three years. Most of the ruins of the old one were washed away in that same great storm which destroyed the Eddystone Lighthouse in 1703, but ever since the tower wall has been kept in repair and painted white as a sea-mark.

The Duver, with its sand dunes and wide green spaces and rare flowers, is a delightful place to ramble, or one can walk across the harbour on the walls of the mill dams, water spreading away on either side and much coming and going of small craft out through the narrow channel leading to that sheltered stretch of water known as St Helen's Roads, for hundreds of years a home to the Fleet. St Helens was an important port by the sixteenth century. Sir John Oglander wrote, "Many ships resorted here to victual, it had a fleet of fifty sail and was home of twenty good ship masters that would undertake to carry you to any port you desired." Nearby, when the English fleet sailed out to fight the French, the *Mary Rose* sank with most of her crew.

Charles II, who had the very first Royal Yacht built, often visited The Roads. In 1671 he actually sailed with the Fleet, but a great storm off St Helens dispersed the ships so that he finally landed in Devon. The following year with the English and French for once united (against the Dutch) he reviewed a combined fleet of over one hundred ships in St Helen's Roads. (In 1945 an even greater fleet assembled here for the invasion of France.)

But as Cowes grew in prosperity, so St Helens, as a port, lost trade: also it had to fight the constant silting up of the harbour. Smuggling and fishing and coal were the maritime trades of the nineteenth century. At the end of the dams is the wharf where the colliers used to unload coal to be trucked away by the "puffer".

A delightful footpath through woods leads from the Duver to St Helens Green, while the road passes an entrance to the Priory. After the old priory down by the sea had disappeared, the monks' farm house took on that title and played an important part in village life. In the eighteenth century the house was much enlarged, in the nineteenth almost rebuilt, by the Grose family. As a country seat of the gentry it employed an army of servants, grooms and gardeners. In the 1930s an American millionairess added an ornate doorway and clock tower, while peacocks and highland cattle roamed amid exotic shrubs.

Just below the Priory lies Old Watch House Point. When the watch house itself was thought to be unsafe, it was pulled down in 1922 by order of the Priory's owner, Miss Spencer Edwards. After her death, two old men came forward and described how, when they were dismantling the watch house, they found a great hoard of church treasure. Miss Spencer Edwards swore them to secrecy and had them cart it up to the Priory cellars. They felt able to speak only because she was now dead. One of them said, "It was mostly church stuff, crucifixes, chalices, small chests of gold and jewellery. Bags of coins and some old books."

Could this be from the real Priory, hidden in haste at rumour of a French raid? Were the books handwritten? One longs to know more, but the treasure has never been seen again. The Priory is now a holiday centre.

St Helens Green is a really vast open space, more than nine acres, a long rectangle with seats along the upper side looking across to Culver Down, and alleys and roads on the lower leading down to the harbour. Houses ring the green in a splendidly varied architectural jumble, Victorian yellow brick villas, semi-detacheds from between the wars, a neo-Georgian garage, two chapels, a scatter of bungalows and between them all, the old cottages of the original village, one beautifully thatched, another actually on the green, bears the date 1681. There used to be two pubs, next door to each other, The Vine and The Sailors Home, but the latter, known as "a real rough old pub", has closed.

(Down toward the sea the houses tend to be grander, with pseudo-Elizabethan gables, turrets, grounds rather than gardens: there is even The Castle, a Victorian house with "Norman" drum towers built on to its corners.)

The village has a quietly prosperous air, remains a working community in no way tarted up. The green, while cared for, is in constant use for cricket, football and kids just playing around. A pond once lay out in the middle with so large a flock of attendant geese that the old local name for the village was Goose Island. Also on the green are nine very old wells, though now all are covered (one is just behind the goalpost), so the green must always have been a meeting place. St Helens has been renowned for the purity of its water: the fleet would come out from Portsmouth and stock up with it, if sailing on a long expedition, because it would keep fresh longer than any other. The well water was analysed in 1930 and found to be purer than that from the mains.

On one of the houses is a plaque to Sophie Dawes: locals will still shake their heads and murmur, "Ah, she was a one," even if Sophie died in 1840. Her father, Dicky Dawes, was, officially, by occupation a fisherman, but really made a living by smuggling. For all that pretty picture of geese on the green and maids by the well, in the eighteenth century St Helens must really have been a rough, tough village, especially in the lower harbour area. The fleet was often in with its camp followers, suppliers and loose women, while local men went in constant fear of the Press Gangs who came ashore looking for strong likely labour to be forced aboard ship. Smuggling was a way of life for labourers and fishermen who could not otherwise support a family.

All kinds of tricks were practised round the island, to keep "nosy parkers" away. At St Helens, one of the gang would drape over himself a white sheet daubed with black paint in the shape of a skeleton, perch on a tombstone down by the harbour and beat out hollow rhythms on a drum! Dicky Dawes would have no truck with such ruses, preferring to rely solely on his seamanship, to keep out of the hands of the Excise: one narrow channel between the rocks is still known as Dicky Dawes Gut.

When he died, the proceeds of this expertise were not enough to keep his family, who were sent to the House of Industry at Newport, but Sophie ran away, first to Portsmouth, then to London where her beauty was noticed by the Duc de Bourbon. He sent Sophie to school and made her his mistress. At the Restoration she followed him to Paris and there led a life of luxury and scandal—a far cry from the barefoot urchin picking winkles for dinner on the reefs of St Helens.

The "new" church was built some way north: the pleasantest way to reach it is along a footpath which turns off the green and winds through fields—about ten minutes' walk. The building, with a wooden bell tower at that time, was consecrated by Bishop Trelawney in 1719, some of the tombstones from the old church being incorporated in the floor. The sanctuary walls bear a dignified collection of memorial tablets mostly to families connected with the Priory, while various hatchments are attached, rather unusually, to the roof beams. St Helena, to whom the church is dedicated, was mother of the Emperor Constantine. A founder of churches, she is best remembered for finding what she claimed to be the true cross, after seeing it in a vision. Evelyn Waugh wrote a novel about her, called *Helena.* A stained-glass window in the north wall depicts St Helena holding the cross, and also St Wilfred. The road back to the green passes Eddington Manor House, preserving a name from Norman times.

You would not easily guess who built a chapel for the village—it was Edward Dawes, Sophie's nephew. In fact he became a much-respected figure, lived in a large house down by the old church and stood as radical member of parliament for the island in 1851, giving rise to the robust election slogan—

Dawes for ever—Hammond in the river,
A knife in his heart and a fork in his liver.

Lovers of the eccentric should not miss the Shell Garden, belonging to a house on the green. Here a long narrow garden bounded by breeze block walls has been transformed by covering every inch of space with a mosaic of shells and bright pottery fragments, interspersed with whole plates or plaques, and more importantly by large murals created, with paint, shingle and stones—a new slant on the village. Here are depicted both the churches, the windmill, a series of tall ships including the *Winston Churchill* sometimes to be seen in St Helen's Roads, and a Romany caravan.

The road past the church leads on to Seaview, with a wide view of the harbour bowered in trees below, and Bembridge Point beyond, or you can walk through the fields, past the gate of the Priory for a last brooding thought on that cartload of treasure.

Seaview has a vast hinterland of new building estates but the older village, near the sea, retains an atmosphere of more leisurely days, with narrow streets and alleyways sloping down to the Solent, framing views of great oil tankers moving up to Fawley, or grey Navy ships out of Portsmouth or bright painted Channel ferries.

In fact none of Seaview is very old. In 1545 the French landed here to attack a fort "which had annoyed their galleys", but this was probably an isolated building guarding the Solent. West of it, marshy land sprawled down to Barnsley Creek which extended toward Pondwell and Nettlestone.

So it was quite a hazardous journey for Brother Martin at St Helen's Priory to visit his orphan niece in Ryde (or La Rye as the village was then called) as he was allowed to do once a week. Legend tells that his habit was first to visit certain comely ladies there. One day, not having left himself time to call on Fanny at all, he was hurrying back to the Priory at dusk, through the marshes, when he heard Fanny herself calling for help from a green island. When he floundered through the mud to it, Fanny was not there, though her voice was calling to him from another part of the marsh, together with another sound, wha-whee, wha-wee, which he could not at first identify till he came upon a row of oysters, rhythmically opening and closing their shells, and he realized they were laughing at him. He never found Fanny, was assailed by crabs, owls and bats, and eventually reached the Priory drenched through and smothered in mud. The Prior accepted his explanation of a fall in the swamps, but whenever Brother Martin again tried to visit one of his comely ladies in La Rye, the oysters' laughter would ring in his ears and he would turn away . . .

Later some salt pans were formed out of the marsh, and the first cottages built in 1640, but the industry did not assume any importance till 1790 when a new and energetic owner enlarged the pans and employed a gang of men to produce salt from brine evaporated by the sun. This could only happen in summer, so in winter the men were employed in building an embankment and sluices to regulate water levels, which meant the end of Barnsley Creek. Salt was of course in great demand as the only method of keeping meat for any period of time, and carried a high duty, bringing its price to a guinea a bushel. Saltern Cottages remain one of the most picturesque corners of the village, one of them housing Seaview Pottery, where the potter can be seen at work.

A café name now commemorates the Old Fort. The real village grew into being only from about 1800, when, according to the local pun, "The cause of Seaview was the Caws". A field called Fort Ground was bought by the Caws family and divided into plots on which they built cottages, and the sea wall. This original plot is now bounded by High Street, Esplanade, West Street and Rope Walk, a long narrow alley where new rope was laid out to be stretched.

The Caws began as a maritime family of fishermen and pilots, but soon, as in Bembridge, Seaview was discovered by those caught up in the new fashion of seaside holidays: the Caws branched out into guest-houses. That enormous pseudo-Tudor pile in the High Street was built by Douglas Caws as estate offices. Better-off visitors—and Seaview always considered itself superior—built their own seaside "cottages" for the summer season. The directory for 1871 describes Seaview as "A picturesquely situated village, a favourite place of resort for those who desire to shun the bustle and gaiety of Ryde. Bathing machines, hot, cold and shower baths etc."

One constraint upon a growing resort was its lack of communications. Before the present toll road was built along the coast, there was only a footpath across the Coney Duver—coney being the old name for a rabbit—so that the only way into the village was by steep and narrow Old Seaview Lane through Nettlestone,

Bembridge Harbour

St Helen's Green

View of the Solent from Seaview

Wootton Creek

A Binstead lane

Longford, now a hospital

Arreton Craft Centre

Haseley Manor

All Saints' Church, Newchurch

The interior of All Saints', Newchurch

Brading Church, Town Hall and Wax Museum

The tomb of Sir John Oglander

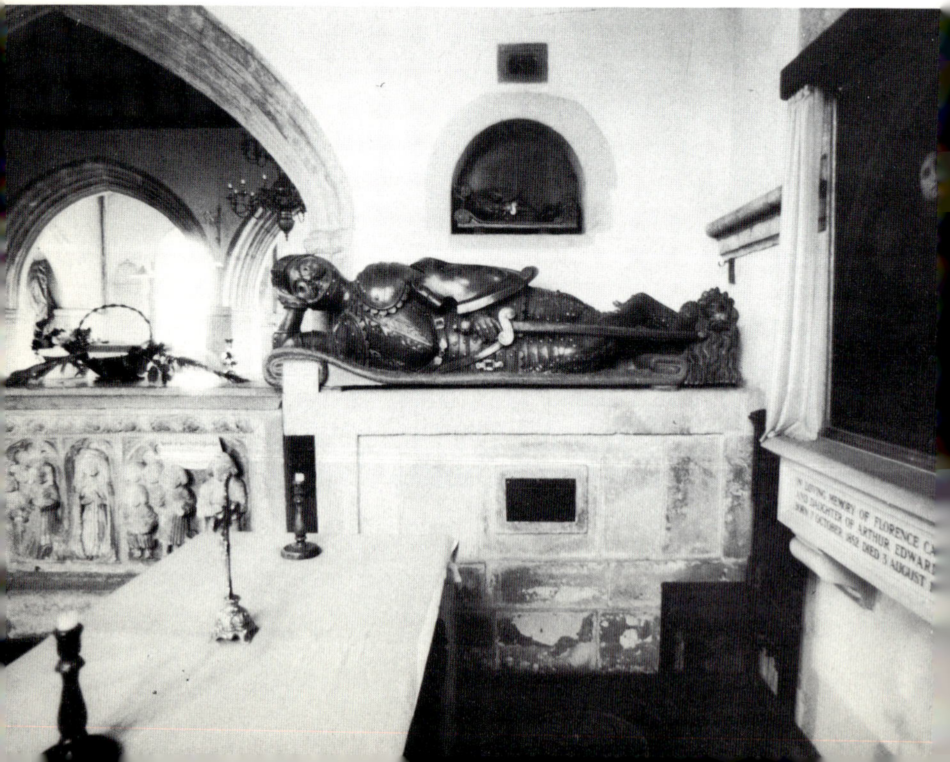

Northwood Church

Mouth of the Luck, Gurnard Marsh

though one other surprising route sometimes offered itself. "Seaview possesses a fine level bed of sand which extends to a considerable distance on each side of the point; firm enough for riding or even driving; so that at a proper state of the tide, the distance from Ryde is considerably diminished by taking a carriage across the sands to Springvale."

Plans to extend a light railway to Seaview came to nothing, but the pier was built in 1880 to supply, as the prospectus said, "a want which had long been felt by the Inhabitants and Visitors who had hitherto been deprived of the advantages possessed by other Watering Places of a Pier for Promenading. It will extend to a distance of about nine hundred feet into the sea. The present extreme low price of iron work offers a most favourable opportunity".

Of course the real benefit of the pier was to provide a direct link with Portsmouth and further boost the holiday trade. No horses, cattle, sheep, pigs, timber, bricks or stone were to be shipped. Tolls for promenading the pier were one penny per person, with an additional penny if accompanied by a dog—and no dog was to be permitted to come out of the water upon the pier except to prevent drowning. Yet another member of the Caws family, Francis, designed the pier, which resembled a suspension bridge in construction. Older inhabitants can remember jumping up and down to make the pier swing. The pilot boats transferred there from the High Street slipway and a large hotel, The Pier, was built on the new esplanade. The Gosport Launch Company used to run excursions from Southsea known locally as "Sixpenny Sickers".

Seaview was in the parish of St Helens so that church-goers had to make their way to that village every Sunday. In 1858 land was given for the present church, built of Swanage stone, but all kinds of squabbles followed its erection and it was not consecrated for many years: in 1902 its patron removed all books and ornaments and the church was locked for some months! The original church, designed by Thomas Hellyer, has been several times enlarged and could easily be mistaken for, say, a church school of Victorian times: it looks its best in April when the cherries and magnolia are out.

Inside, the twentieth-century addition of a south aisle has resulted in a church of unusual width: the nave is enclosed by low brick-lined arches and separated from the sanctuary by a striking wrought-iron screen. Florence Barcley, author of the famous Victorian novel *The Rosary*, used to worship here. One day, her mind straying from the sermon, she spent a long time gazing at the East Window which depicts St Peter. The plot of her next novel involved a stone smashing through this window: it was called *The Broken Halo*.

When larger and more comfortable boats began a regular ferry service from Portsmouth to Ryde, the pier's prosperity declined. It was closed on the outbreak of war in 1939 and finally destroyed in great storms during the last week of 1951. "At midnight it was as if a hurricane were raging, as tremendous waves swept masses of pier timbers onto the esplanade. At the height of the storm both toll kiosks were lifted bodily and even an iron turnstile was flung across the esplanade."

And more than thirty years later the scene at the foot of Pier Road is again desolate and rubble strewn. The Pier Hotel was pulled down and replaced by the modern Halland Hotel—then this too was demolished. Plans for yet another hotel have just fallen through and so a vast empty space remains, with a pleasant stretch of sea wall leading on to quiet footpaths down to Seagrove Bay, the more secluded end of the village, with a wide, crumbling sea wall coming to an end just short of the wooded point, cutting off from sight Priory Bay where once a watch of ten men by day and four by night kept a beacon ready to fire in case of invaders from France.

Now invasion comes from inland as the new housing estates march ever nearer the sea.

The point itself is called Horestone, but on old maps, Orestone: some of the boulders are that fierce orange-brown betraying the presence of iron. Were they ever gathered for smelting, as the name seems to imply, like similar stones at the foot of Hengistbury Head? Bamboo and willow grow behind the sea wall, evidence of seeping water which has eaten away foundations and finally destroyed several houses along this stretch of coast.

Earlier this century Seagrove Bay was lined with bathing tents, some on the sea wall, while the beach itself sometimes became an aerodrome! In 1921 a Captain Dalton began to advertise the latest in modern motoring, the Cubitt Two Seater, price £435, trial runs available at the Aerodrome—which was actually the sands at low tide! From here the captain also ran joy rides in small aeroplanes.

The grounds of various mansions built in Seaview's heyday have been largely split up into building plots, but many of the high stone walls surrounding them remain an interesting feature. Today the village has a variety of shops including Bookworm, several for yachting clothes and a quality shoe shop founded in 1860 by yet another Caws and still run by the family. Yacht clubs and boat builders continue to flourish, while the newest sport is the school of wind surfing, off the Duver.

Behind the Duver, another new development is Saltern Holiday Bungalows, grouped round a lawn looking toward the sea, their low roofs already patched with that golden lichen which will grow only in clean air. From the grounds one can look across the old saltern channels and marshes, haunt of swans and moorhen whilst listening to peacock and other exotic cries from Flamingo Park.

This bird sanctuary, inspired by Peter Scott's Slimbridge, was established in 1971 on a wide slope of land just west of Seaview. Though begun with pairs of pinioned birds, these have bred free-flying young, so that a flock of macaws, green winged, scarlet, military or blue and gold, may be flying overhead. Twenty black swans are all the progeny of the original pair and the geese have had similar breeding success, increasing by over a hundred—varieties include barnacle, Egyptian and snow goose. Only the flamingo themselves, elegant and superior looking on their stilt legs, have so far refused to breed.

The latest addition is a larger semi-tropical house where soft bills such as laughing thrushes and exotically coloured starlings fly free among palm trees, rubber plants and beds of flowers, to the sound of waterfalls. This means that visitors can wander among birds whatever the weather.

While the bathing machines have long disappeared, Seaview still "shuns the bustle and gaiety of Ryde". The same families return year after year to their favourite houses and plots of beach: no through traffic breaks the Edwardian charm of its seaboard.

2

The North East

The thousands of motorists who drive through Wootton on the main road from Ryde to Newport might well dismiss the place as a ribbon of modern red brick broken only by the creek, when in fact it is one of the island's oldest settlements.

Once off the busy road, various leafy, unadopted lanes lead out towards the coast. Finally, a footpath down through oak woods leads to the Solent shore, a little sandy beach with spectacular views across to Portsmouth and Ryde Pier. From the evidence of axes and arrow heads this was a Mesolithic settlement, its people hunting small prey in the woods and gathering shellfish from the rocks.

Now the coastal woods shelter a different kind of settlement, several holiday camps. The newest development is Aquaview Village, a group of holiday villas with a delightful view across the creek to the wooded east bank and its own small inlet where mallard dive between anchored dinghies. Aquaview differs from the holiday camps in its time ownership scheme.

Through a maze of new suburban roads, redeemed somewhat by many trees and glimpses of the creek below, one comes to St Edmund's Church, ancient and unadorned.

At the time of the Domesday survey, Wootton was known as Odetone, the farm by the wood, and valued at three pounds. It was "held of the honour of Carisbrooke by the service of finding a horseman for the defence of the Isle of Wight in time of war, and doing suit at the court of Knights at Newport every three weeks". By the thirteenth century it belonged to the de Insula family who were to be part of Wootton history for five hundred years, their name changing form, though not meaning, to de L'isle and finally Lisle.

At this time the main crops were barley, wheat, oats and peas, while the farm stock included twenty ploughing oxen, some four hundred sheep and eight peacocks.

Walter de Insula built the church in the eleventh century, probably for his own family worship; later a chantry was added on the north side. Tradition says it was burned down some three hundred years later, but there is still a finely carved south doorway and plain Norman nave. In the vestry, which now takes the place of the chantry, the list of rectors begins with "Edmund de Lisle 1283", the list of chantry priests ends, "1535 Edward Banyon, 1536, chantry dissolved".

A small wooden figure of Christ looks down from the rood beam and there is a handsomely carved Jacobean pulpit.

Even though the creek opened into the sheltered waters of the Solent it was always felt to be vulnerable. In 1324, Sir John de Insula, Keeper of Ports and Shores reported that a watch was kept at Wootton Point with an alarm beacon ready to be lit. Wootton Farm is the site of the de Insulas' medieval manor house. Henry VII paid a visit there to see Sir Nicholas Lisle and one hopes he was royally entertained; for a later Lisle, Sir William, was described as one of the best housekeepers in the island, but after a homely, slovenly way because of differences between him and his wife!

During the Civil War the majority of islanders supported Cromwell, even when King Charles was imprisoned in Carisbrooke Castle, but a Captain Burley, who lived in Newport, raised a mob with the intention of marching on the castle and freeing the king. He was arrested, taken to Wootton and there hung, drawn and quartered as due warning to other islanders with similar intent.

Lisles continued to be lords of the manor till the eighteenth century, when other large houses and estates began to appear. One of these was Fernhill, a mansion in Gothic style with a high tower, built on the west bank of the creek by Thomas Orde Powlett, later Governor of the Wight. This must have been one of the most beautiful estates on the island, its grounds, planted with ornamental trees sweeping right down to the bridge, included an observatory, boathouses, an ice house, summer-houses and a conservatory, while part of it was farmed. In 1794 Earl Howe won a great naval victory over the French. "No displays of animated ardour at this period of celebration, have exceeded those at Fernhill. The house with its aspiring gothic tower was adorned with more than a thousand lamps of powerful lustre. The lawns and gardens were crowded with respectable parties . . . and within doors hospitality loaded the table with every kind of substantial and delicate refreshment."

Various distinguished island families occupied Fernhill till 1958 when, during building works to turn it into flats, the house caught fire and was destroyed: now the garden is a caravan site, the grounds built over, but remains of this estate which covered half of Wootton can still be traced. Down the turning off Station Road, called Fernhill, part of a great ivied wall still stands beside the stone gateposts of the carriage entrance and beyond lie the stables and coachhouse, while among the caravans stand some fine mature cedars.

The other entrance by the bridge, now the drive to Lakeside, led also to the farmhouse, now called Froggats, occupied for many years by C. A. Joyce the well-known broadcaster.

While the gentry built mansions, ordinary village life continued to revolve round the farms and the quay: even today the bridge seems the heart of the village. Southwards the creek broadens into a wide lake below sloping green banks of fields and woods, while northwards it winds between boatyards and houseboats towards the sea. Here the banks are covered with modern buildings but largely bowered in trees so that the overall effect is still green and pretty in summer—trees are the scenic salvation of Wootton.

The bridge was originally the causeway of a dam built for the tide mill which stood here beside the pub. A survey of 1794 says: "The island's fertility is almost proverbial, having long since been said to produce more in one year than could be consumed by the inhabitants in eight." Grain was the chief crop then, but by Victorian times, corn was being imported and barges from Southampton docked at Mill Quay bringing cargoes to be ground into flour which was then sent out round the island by wagon. Part of the mill was once used as a school, later as a post office. After it was converted to steam power, the village women used to call in on Monday mornings to take away surplus hot water for washday: later the machinery was converted to gas, then to diesel.

The quay was the working heart of the village: Wootton Coal Company brought in frequent cargoes, as did Wootton Trading Company. The *Solent Goose* brought all kinds of cargoes from Portsmouth and Southampton, including beer for the pub. Altogether the quay was a tough quarter: fights were sometimes held in a makeshift boxing ring in the mill, with flour sacks as posts.

At those same Fernhill naval celebrations, "It would be unjust to omit the exertions of Mr Vick, an eminent miller at Wootton Bridge. Ingenuity and loyalty concurred in the disposition of brilliant ornaments in his house and gardens which reflected from the water had the effect of almost magical enchantment." The mill ceased working at the end of the last war and was pulled down in 1962.

Next to its site stands The Sloop, which used to be the half-way coach stop between Ryde and Newport. Now you can eat a variety of home-made snacks on a patio splendidly placed for watching the coming and going of boats and swans on the creek.

Opposite lies Lakeside, a leisure park where you can eat and drink on the more rural bank of the creek, looking across to Firestone Copse and the old farmhouse of Kitehill, recently restored, or take a rowing boat out on the creek itself and explore its peaceful and unspoilt waters.

The High Street, sloping steeply up from the bridge is lined with shops and modern houses. The latest development here has been to convert the old Conservative Hall into a shopping arcade, to complement, rather than compete with, existing traders, and provide a café, all to be known as Bumble's Lane. This sounds like the revival of some charming old local name; in fact the new arcade is named after the Rector's sheep-dog!

The parish is a very scattered one, though not as far-flung as when it included the village of Chillerton on the other side of Newport some eight miles away. In a directory for 1871 the population, including Chillerton, is given as sixty-nine, the only trades mentioned being farmer, yacht and boat builder, van and cart wheelwrights. "Scarcely more populated than a clearing in the backwoods of America," one writer remarked. Now, with a population of hundreds, a bus goes the rounds on Sundays, to pick up the faithful for church, St Edmund's being some way from the centre.

But there is also a "new" church, built that is in 1910, opposite the lodge to Fernhill. Anyone with a tendency to despise twentieth-century churches should pay it a visit. Certainly from the outside, St Mark's resembles a church hall but the inside is really striking, built of red brick, like the new church at Quarr, very light and spacious with an elegant curved altar rail.

All the time the creek draws one's eye and the trying thing about Wootton is that no public paths lead along beside it. At Mill Quay you can look across at boatbuilders' yards, but to enjoy the creek itself turn right just past the bridge and make for Firestone Copse.

Firestone is mixed woodland sloping down westwards, managed by the Forestry Commission: for years there were gravelled tracks round it, but recently the Commission have made many alterations, first of all creating a large parking and picnicking area by the road, and then, with real imagination, they have cleared and laid a path right down by the head of the creek. One can wander along by the water's edge but still just inside the copse, ideal for bird watching.

In spring there are little wild daffodils, and later lungwort can be found. Please don't pick them: they look so beautiful growing naturally beneath the oaks and hazels.

East of Wootton and merging into it lies Fishbourne, leading down the eastern bank of the creek. At the time of the French raids along the south coast, this eastern point was known as Fish House, where the abbot of nearby Quarr Abbey was licensed to build stone fortifications. Later a watch of two men was always kept, with a beacon fire ready to be lit to raise the alarm. More recently a coastguard station was maintained here.

Fishbourne was also known for its boatyards. In 1815 the Fleming estate leased some two hundred and fifty yards of creek frontage to James and David List, at an annual rent of six pounds ten shillings, for a shipyard, reserving out of this grant, "all manner of timber trees and other trees—young heirs and saplings and the bodies of all pollards now standing or growing . . . with free liberty to cart and carry away at their wills and pleasures."

A guide book of 1844 notes that "the noblest yachts which have graced the Squadron at Cowes were launched from the yard of Mr D. List at Fishbourne".

From the time of the monks, boats plied between here and the mainland. In 1817 the rate was five shillings and sixpence for one passenger and not exceeding four, from Portsmouth to Fish House, plus one shilling for a return journey (it was sixpence more to be taken right up to Wootton Bridge). These were the fine weather fares, "to be increased by one half when the Blue Flag was hoisted, and doubled in foul weather when the red triangle was hoisted".

Today this otherwise quiet, residential road houses the British Rail Car Ferry Terminal from Portsmouth. Its vast yard sloping down to the creek handles rail freight containers and a large commercial trade as well as cars. The latest ferries, which island people always refer to as "boats", look clumsy and unwieldy with their broad roll on-roll off bows, but they are very easy for the motorist to cope with and comfortable for passengers too.

Hidden away down a lane lies Ranalagh Boat Yard which offers every facility to visiting yachtsmen, while next door to the ferry stands the Royal Victoria Yacht Club with lawns to the water's edge.

Fishbourne Point is a delightful spot, a circular green surrounding one great oak tree, with glimpses of the creek mouth beyond. One of the houses, lying back from the lane and bowered in trees, is called The Watch House. Along the Solent shore, past boathouses and another little green, stand the old coastguard cottages.

A lane leads to Binstead, passing through the ruins of Old Quarr, and the drive of the new abbey.

Binstead resembles Wootton in shape, a red-brick High Street sloping steeply downhill, but with a mere stream at the bottom rather than a creek. In fact the road seems to slice the village in halves, the old near the sea, the new to the south. You might well guess that the village sprang into being round the monastery of Quarr whose ruins lie in the sea meadows, but it is far older, owing its existence to the hard limestone which outcrops here and has been quarried for two thousand years.

A Roman altar found at Bitterne, near Southampton, was made of Binstead stone and so were parts of Portchester Castle. In the Domesday survey the village is called Benestede, though the abbey took its name from the quarries. In 1293 an inquisition was taken at Swanestone (Swainston) "as to whether it will be to the injury of the King if he permits the Abbot Quarrera to dig and take away stone for the fabric of his church at Quarrera". The jury found the quarry of the King at Benestede sufficient for the fabric of the Abbot's church "and all works which the King will have wished to make in the said island".

Later the stone was used in the building of Chichester Cathedral, Netley and Beaulieu Abbeys and the restoration of Winchester by William of Wykeham, as well as many smaller churches. When Warblington Castle was rebuilt by the Countess of Salisbury in Tudor times, some Quarr stone was used costing eightpence a ton. By the nineteenth century the best of the stone was largely worked out, though the Newport to Ryde road was surfaced with chippings from Quarr Pit in 1814, by which time it cost one shilling (5p) per wagonload: many of the old abandoned workings were already overgrown.

However, the quarries were still useful. Smuggling was rife by then even in the Solent: bales of lace and silk brought in to Wootton Creek from France could be conveniently hidden away under gorse and bracken in the old pits. A small seam of stone was opened up at the beginning of the century, west of the church, but it is remarkable how little evidence is left of the removal of thousands of tons of stone, north of the road. You can trace out old names still, such as The Pitts.

The original Quarr Abbey, founded in 1132, had to be something of a fortress as well as a house of God. By the fourteenth century, when French raids were constantly feared, the Abbot declared that he should not be expected to fund a ship prepared for war *and* sixty men and full supplies, as he already maintained ten men at arms and no small number of archers.

Though hunting was forbidden to the monks, they were not above poaching. One Brother Hardekyn was sorely tempted by rabbits, which he shot with a bow and arrow. After he had provided rabbit pie three days running, the Abbot challenged him with hunting, but Brother Hardekyn vowed that he kept a pair of tame rabbits in his cell, adding smugly, "their increase is singularly blessed". So he was let off that time, but later caught arrow in hand. This is all documented in the rolls of Ashey Manor.

After the dissolution, much of the abbey stone was carted away and only a few fragments remain in the fields, but a new abbey was built early this century, its rosy towers rising from the surrounding woods. The monks of this Benedictine community spend a large part of each day in study and worship, but each also practises manual work, such as carpentry, weaving and book binding, or helps in the running of the gardens, orchards and farm.

One may visit the abbey, though only the south side of the vast complex of red-brick buildings is visible, and the abbey church services are open to all.

The main road with its constant traffic hardly invites one to saunter around, though it is worth finding the Fleming Arms since it takes its name from a family which has owned land here for hundreds of years: the family motto "Tenax et Fidelis" appears on the inn sign together with the crest emblazoned with lions and owls. Close by the big Island Bakeries, which supply the whole island, are hardly attractive buildings but they do fill the street with delicious smells of newly baked bread. Behind it lie new housing estates and several small factories making electrical parts and cosmetics, so that this area feels more like a suburb of nearby Ryde than a village.

But cross the main road, take a lane leading north and at once the noise of traffic fades away: all is green and enchanting. Narrow lanes wind, between old stone walls overhung with limes and oaks, towards the sea. Through stone arches or between high pillars come glimpses of gardens and rose arbours, sunken glades and grottoes, a twisted chimney, or a thatched roof. It is difficult to realize that much of this pleasantly undulating character is due to the old quarry workings beneath, so green and leafy it appears now. Eastward, Ladies Walk leads towards Ryde, westward a lane meanders past a farmhouse incorporating some ruins of old Quarr.

Horace Smith, a minor nineteenth-century poet, was chiefly famous for his wicked parodies of contemporary poets, especially Wordsworth, but here he was moved to write for himself:

Farewell, sweet Binstead! take a fond farewell
From one unused to sight of woods and trees,
Amid the strife of cities doomed to dwell,
Yet roused to ecstacy by scenes like these;
Who could forever sit beneath thy trees,
Inhaling fragrance from the flowery dell.

The lanes lead eventually to the church which is long and low, hung about with tall trees, with the Solent waters beyond. Some of the gravestones have been rearranged round the outer walls and roses planted in their stead, but the more interesting remain in place, including one carved with a sloop in full sail, often mistakenly called the Smuggler's Grave. The worn and lichened inscription reads, "To the memory of Thomas Sivell who was cruelly shot on board his sloop by some officers of the customs of the Port of Portsmouth, June 1785." In fact Thomas was an innocent man merely sailing his own boat.

The church which looks so ancient and undisturbed has a chequered history. No one knows the exact date of its founding, but parts of it date from Norman times: it was originally a nave without any aisles, but this was demolished in 1844 when the church had sunk into a ruinous condition. While there is some Norman herring-bone masonry in the chancel, the church was practically rebuilt in 1844, the design of Thomas Hellyer. Then in 1969 a serious fire destroyed much of the roof and west end.

But all has been so lovingly restored and improved, one would never guess. The new hammer beams of oak from Sussex made by Moreys of Newport, reproduce the old ones. The treasures of Binstead range from carved stone figures so old they may be heathen gods, to elegant stained-glass windows, inserted after the fire in 1970.

Binstead was at one time included in the parish of Calbourne, and later of Newchurch. The ledger kept by the Overseers of the Poor gives inside information on the life of the times—in this case the Napoleonic Wars. In 1795 the parish was ordered to raise two able-bodied men to serve as volunteers in His Majesty's Navy. "We the church warders do in obedience offer a bounty of thirty two pounds." The parish poor rate having been fixed at sixpence in the pound for one quarter, there had to be paid out seventy-five pounds to the House of Industry, or workhouse, at Newport, and ten shillings Bridewell Money—this was to help maintain the gaol.

In the winter of 1801, parish relief was given to the poor in herrings as well as money, because provisions were so dear; a gallon loaf cost three and sevenpence halfpenny (18p), potatoes eightpence (3½p) a bushel, a pound of pork ten shillings (50p). By 1805, bread had gone down to two and sixpence (12½p). Poor relief was then "to those having large families all above three children under twelve years, one shilling per head".

Beyond the church, where the lanes peter out, a path leads down through the woods, beside a stream to the shore. Certainly the beach is largely mud, shingle and boulders and one cannot walk far along it, but there are no holiday camps in sight, only peaceful woods behind, and ahead ships moving up to Southampton.

Havenstreet lies on higher ground above the head of Wootton Creek: perhaps it was the land known as Strete in the fourteenth century, given to the Abbey of Montebourg by William de Estur—the idea of his wife Joan. The earliest form of the name is Hethenstrete, which could refer to an ancient, pre-Roman track, formed by the feet of the "heathen". It is also suggested that the creek below was once much larger, bringing the village close enough to be called a Haven. The most likely, if less interesting, derivation seems to be a track across heath land.

The village has few really old buildings, consisting mainly of brick houses and cottages, squared off and strung along the road and certainly it hardly grew to village status till the last century, yet the area is full of history. During the making of the railway line a hoard of fourth-century coins was unearthed. Nearby Briddlesford Copse is the site of a lost medieval village, while south east there once stood Ashey Monastery, established by Edward I as a branch of Wherwell Abbey near Andover in

Hampshire. "This monastery of wealth and repute contained a spacious hall, noble refectory and chambers richly decorated."

By 1752 there was a carpenter and wheelwright: old stone work to the rear of the White Hart perhaps represents an older pub, but it was the coming of the railway, and the advent of John Rylands which transformed Havenstreet.

The Newport to Ryde line, passing through the village, with a station built just west of it, was the second steam line to be opened on the island. It opened in 1875 as a passenger service and also did a thriving trade as a goods line transporting coal from Medina Wharf which lay on the river beside Newport station. Closed by British Rail in 1966, the station is now the headquarters of the Isle of Wight Steam Railway, which runs trains to Wootton at weekends.

John Rylands, born in 1801, belonged to a Lancashire cotton family. When they bought a new works at Wigan, the land beneath was found to be rich in coal, which helped swell profits and a branch was opened in London. When his elder brothers retired, John took over the firm, built new mills and travelled abroad setting up a world-wide trade, till Rylands was the largest textile manufacturer in Britain. He lived at Longford Hall, Stretford, where he was a magistrate, and benefactor, building a town hall, library and baths. Elsewhere he founded orphanages and homes for the aged. Visiting Rome, he was so appalled at the poverty of its back streets that he set aside many thousands for the relief of the poor—in fact for this work he was awarded the order of The Crown of Italy, by the King. His money saved the Manchester Ship Canal when it was about to founder through lack of funds.

And John Rylands came to Havenstreet. Deciding to build a house for himself there, he bought up a large part of the land and proceeded to improve the village. He established a gas works beside the station, with cottages for the workers, to supply the area. Though the gasometer has gone, the Gas House still stands by the station yard. Bowered in ivy, windows broken, the tall gabled building resembles a dilapidated chapel, though John Rylands' monogram and the date 1886 can still be seen on the front. House martins have taken over the manager's house, but the workers' cottages are still lived in.

This was a minor scheme, like Longford Cottages right in the village. Opposite the pub stands a vast Victorian pile, a great square red-brick building with an imposing Greek temple entrance and arched windows picked out in yellow brick, which dwarfs everything in sight. John Ryland built the Longford Institute for the villagers: inside they were offered a library, reading rooms, billiard rooms, a lecture hall—all the facilities of a twentieth-century Community Centre. Whatever did the small nineteenth-century farming village make of it? Later it became a temperance hotel, a carriage and then bus depot, a nursing home: now it is the White Owl Restaurant, specializing in a continental cuisine. The erstwhile school building is now the Community Centre.

While the Institute sits hugely by the village street, it is itself dwarfed by the house which Rylands built for himself, further west. Made of stone with vast wings spreading out either side of a high gable, surmounted with turrets, the lofty roof is capped with an observatory: this is now Longford Hospital. Rylands' widow, Enriqueta, founded the famous Rylands Library in Manchester, in memory of her husband.

Havenstreet is a working village: there are two farms along the street. Conspicuously lacking in thatch-and-roses it makes no effort to be picturesque but is set in beautiful, unspoilt country: lanes and footpaths beckon in all directions, some north to Firestone Copse and the creek, others to Combley Great Wood and Rowlands Wood. One lane leads to the church of St Peter, built in 1852 on land given by the Fleming family, when it cost £570. A long low stone building with mellow orange tiles and bell turret, it lies amid trees with every appearance of having been there for hundreds of years—there are even quite sizable yew trees in the churchyard. Designed, like the restored Binstead, by Thomas Hellyer, the interior is equally pleasing.

No one should leave Havenstreet without visiting its unusual war memorial. At the east end of the village a footpath leads up a steep grassy knoll. On its summit a low stone wall encloses a small courtyard and within a stone building houses an altar between slate tablets commemorating the dead of Binstead and Havenstreet. Though other memorials have since been added, the shrine was originally erected by the Fleming family in memory of a son killed in Egypt in 1916, and all those from Binstead and Havenstreet who died in the 1914 war.

From the steps, though the hill is only two hundred feet high, a lovely wide view extends from the southern downs across undulating green farmlands eastward round to the tall spire of All Saints', in Ryde, soaring above the trees, and right across the Solent to Portsmouth and the hills beyond, while down in the valley close by lies that ancient and storied place, Ninham.

A guide book written a hundred years ago describes this view and adds a mention of "Aldermoor Windmill, picturesquely perched on high ground". What a pity this has long vanished, but Ninham Farm remains as evidence of the far older manor then called Newnham, which is mentioned in twelfth-century records as belonging to Quarr Abbey. The grange, or corn store, of Newnham was bought by John Mill (the vandal who broke up the abbey ruins) at the dissolution, and later owned by the Fleming family.

The present farmhouse is partly Tudor but much altered in succeeding centuries—one wall bears the date 1774. Long ago, an Abbot of Quarr is said to have bestowed a special gift on the tenants of the farm. Because he had been a constant and welcome visitor there for many years, they were to have the right of taking the first crop of hay in alternate years from these fields near Ryde called Monks Meads, so long as they preserved at the farm the stone statue of an abbot of Quarr, a reminder of how the abbey's influence spread out over Wootton, Binstead and Havenstreet.

3

Along the East Yar Valley

The eastern Yar winds through the finest agricultural land on the island, flat, fertile, and sheltered from north winds by the central ridge of chalk downs, so along it lie not only some of the oldest villages, such as Arreton and Brading, but a whole concentration of beautiful old houses—some manors, some working farms.

Up on Arreton Down, Bronze Age barrows have revealed pottery, axes and daggers from the earliest inhabitants of Arreton, Neolithic man. Later the Saxons used the same mounds as burial places. But the Romans have left behind a place for the living.

There are eight Roman villa sites on the island and many more places where Roman coins, middens and settlements have been found. Combley Villa, first mentioned in the *Gentleman's Magazine* of 1867, lies nearly at the foot of the downs north of Arreton. Recent excavations have shown it to have been an aisled villa with an adjacent bath house, a large courtyard and a barn or storehouse. The walls were built of Bembridge limestone and flints, except where exceptional strength was needed, for corner-stones for example, when a very heavy stone conglomerate was brought down from the top of the hill where it outcrops—discarded chunks of it still lie around in the grass. For the domed bath house ceiling where a lighter material was needed, the Roman builders used that spongy-looking stone called tufa.

Though the bath house must have had copious water supplies, no conduits have been found so perhaps wooden ones have rotted away, but it was floored with a dolphin mosaic. The entrance had a geometric design on its floor. The rear of the villa was built on running sand and here these extraordinarily skilled builders had shored up the walls with massive wooden piles. But there was one difficulty on site which they could not overcome and this probably led to the abandonment of the villa—the land is frequently waterlogged.

The villa seems to have been vacated in a peaceful, orderly way—a great pity from the archaeologist's point of view. (A hurried departure means much more is left behind in the way of jewellery and pots.) Later the Saxons built a dwelling across one corner of the ruin, but this was made of chalk from the down which frost flakes away.

Down in the broad Vale, the first mention of a settlement is in King Alfred's will of 885, where it is called Eaderingtune. At first glance today's village hardly seems old; a mere ribbon of building, much of this century, along a main road. But pause at the White Lion, for behind it lies the nucleus of the real Arreton.

Tradition says a wooden church, built by St Wilfred's converts, stood here as early as the eighth century. At the Norman Conquest the church was given to the Abbey of Lyra in Normandy, then to Quarr Abbey. The monks built a farmhouse, a great barn and set about enlarging the church, and behind the pub, sheltered by the down above and bowered in trees, here is their farm, their grange and pond and the church, ancient and full of treasures. Massive buttresses support the walls and the squat tower resembles a fort.

Inside there is an instant impression of light and space, though the remaining Saxon and Norman windows are small and deeply set. A range of portholes above the arches were once the windows of a clerestory, put in to lighten the nave when the tower, built in 1299, blocked the east window, but these in turn were covered by eighteenth-century roof extensions. Two sculptured heads at the juncture of the southern arches are thought to be the Abbot and his master mason, though their small size makes them resemble children.

One of the oldest monuments is a brass set in the sanctuary floor, to Harry Hawles, "Long tyme steward of the Yle of Wight", who fought at Agincourt in 1415. On the tower wall hang boards commemorating various founders of local charities, such as Richard Gard of Princelade who left ten shillings annually to be distributed to the poor on All Saints' Day.

The oak chest dated 1639 has three locks, two for the church-wardens' keys, one for the vicar's, and all must be turned together. Near it lie the remains of a thirteenth-century font and fragments of stone figures including a dragon's head.

Outside there are monuments to William Colnet (said to be a relation of the last Emperor of Constantinople), to Oliver Cromwell's grandson William, and to Legh Richmond's heroine, the Dairyman's Daughter. The churchyard ghost must date from the Civil War period: it is said to be a boy who races up the steps and hammers on the church door crying, "Sanctuary, sanctuary!"

The oldest rooms in the nearby Arreton Manor incorporate part of the monks' original farmhouse. A gracious, symmetrical, stone, largely Elizabethan house with a later porch, it is open to the public and incorporates the National Wireless Museum, a gallery of period dolls and dolls' houses, an agricultural museum, shops and a café.

Doubtless in Stuart times the owner sported with his fellow squires, for their playground was on his doorstep. Twice a week, they would meet at a club house on the slope of St George's Down, to dine and play cards or bowls, "a merry gang of gentlemen that loved a cup of sack and a pretty girl", though Edward Cheke of Merstone, another manor in Arreton parish, "was a brave noble gentleman, and a good seaman and fellow, but an ill husband".

In the middle of this century, the outbuildings of Arreton Manor Farm fell into disuse. Stables, four feet deep in vintage dung, stood among head-high nettles and a sea of mud from the overflowing pond: now all this has been recently transformed into Arreton Craft Centre. The rambling cart sheds and stables have been turned into a series of self-contained workshops without losing the rural atmosphere of rough wood and stone.

When the enterprise was opened, five crafts were displayed, but every year more dilapidated corners have been restored, more workshops opened, so that the range now extends from butterfly jewellery to a thirteen-foot yawl. The forge is currently restoring a vintage steam engine and a copper weather-vane: next door the boatyard is turning out kits for the Whitboat Welker. The products of the wood shop range from bookends to benches and tables, while the smaller studios house portrait drawing, leather work, a print shop, restoration of rocking horses, a flute maker, knitting, pottery and ornamental candles.

One can wander about at will, watch the craftsmen at work, perhaps buy a picture in leather which you saw being created. Prices are reasonable since no middleman is involved. Of course the kinds of craft change from year to year and the centre continues to expand. The next job of restoration, and the most challenging of all, is the ruined barn which dates from the fourteenth century, built by the monks to house their corn. A temporary covering will be the first step, but even the roof timbers have collapsed now. The long-term aim is to reinstate the barn as a centre for village life, to use it to house the Harvest Home supper for example, as it used to do.

Church meetings used to be held in the thatched cottage by the church, at one time called Stile House. The Red Lion has disappeared, but the White Lion remains. Old drawings of it, deep thatched behind trees, show the pub as part of this picturesque group of old Arreton, but as early as 1912 it was being dragged into the twentieth century, for a guide of that time says, "The White Lion is of some antiquity, though many additions have lately been made, greatly to the detriment of its original quaintness and simplicity."

Arreton is an unusual village in that it contains four major tourist attractions yet makes no concessions—no Pixie Tea Gardens, prettied-up guest-houses or Ye Olde souvenir shops. It continues to make a living from the land: the Vale of Arreton is a vegetable basket for the whole island. Field upon reddish field stretch away, acres of potatoes, Brussels sprouts, peas, cabbages, in their season: though the fields are larger now and crops may vary, this land has been cultivated for hundreds of years. Old directories point up ancillary jobs which have now disappeared, such as wheelwright and blacksmith.

In Victorian times, who needed shops outside the village, when the post office was also "grocer, provision dealer, seed, china, earthenware, meal and ironmongery establishment"? Also at Staplers, then in the parish, lived George Tucker, "export perfumer and manufacturer of the Isle of Wight Sauce".

Along the lane over St George's Down which was once the main road to Newport, and others which branch off westward, can be found various fine old houses such as East and West Standen, Merston Manor, Hale Manor, Stickworth Hall and Horringford. None of these is open to the public but can be enjoyed as part of this unspoilt rural landscape.

While Arreton Manor and its vicinity would seem to be Britain's most richly haunted corner, it is from the down above that strange cries echo, howling as of wolves and eldritch screeches. Tucked away up there lies another tourist attraction, Robin Hill Country Park, though islanders are frequent visitors too.

The latest addition to the park's attractions—free-range animals, assault course, woodland walks—is the Chelonian Project. In an attractive jungly setting of small pools, rocks and rubber plants, all a-flicker with little bright-plumaged tropical birds, drowses a large collection of turtles and tortoises, ranging from ash-tray to meat-dish size. This is a long-term, non-commercial project to study the successful maintenance and breeding of the turtle family whose numbers in the wild are becoming much reduced.

Combley Roman Villa lies within the grounds of Robin Hill. Its mosaic floors have had to be reburied to preserve them, but it must be the only place in Britain where the archaeologist can look up from the study of a Roman tile to meet the benevolent gaze of a wallaby. Coyotes and peacocks are responsible for most of the strange cries.

Though the village now straggles from Arreton Manor to Haseley Manor down by the old railway line, Haseley was once a settlement in its own right and is listed as a lost medieval village. A much newer settlement is Haseley Combe, a small council estate and worth looking at as a model of its kind. Houses built of artificial stone, grouped round a circular close, form a pleasant, traffic-free part of the village.

Probably the first dwelling here on the bank of the Yar was a thatched Saxon farmhouse, called Haesel-leak, or Hazelwood: already a prosperous estate it was given, like Arreton, to Quarr Abbey in 1136. Picture Haseley then, with the downs a vast sheep run. The monks built a great wool room on to the house, with a mill beside it for fulling the fleeces: they dug fish ponds and made a road arrowing straight to the north and the mother house at Quarr.

At the Dissolution of the Monasteries, Quarr was pulled down with indecent speed and some of its stone used by the Mill family, its new owners, to rebuild Haseley. Then it was bought by the Flemings who were to own it for more than three hundred years, putting in large Georgian windows when these became fashionable and later adding Victorian bays. In this century, part was split up into farm workers' cottages.

By 1976 Haseley was derelict, overgrown with ivy, riddled with woodworm, leaking and unloved in a jungle of weeds and bramble. Today it is restored and open to the public, a fascinating place to visit simply because it is such a jumble of styles. On the grand scale there are the Norman timbers of the wool room, now a museum, and the fireplace, big enough to roast a whole ox, which takes up one entire wall of the kitchen: the maids' bedroom provides simpler domestic detail—six truckle beds could be pushed into alcoves under the eaves and a hole cut in the door would betray forbidden candlelight.

The fish pond now provides a moat for a children's play-castle and the monks' road is a straight green way up on to the downs, whilst the cart shed houses a working pottery.

During the recent renovations an extraordinary mummified cat was found under the floor, thought to have been a superstitious offering by the Tudor builders. But it is not a cat which haunts Haseley. Several visitors have met a swarthy man in Tudor costume, head thrown back in laughter. When Dowsabell Mill was widowed, she took as her lover Sir Edward Horsey, Governor of the Island: at Haseley they entertained royally, a week's housekeeping including, "one or two beefs, eight sheep, two quarters of wheat and malt, with all things else proportionable". Sir Edward was renowned for his generous and cheerful temperament . . .

Later the Newport to Sandown railway ran close by, with a station at Horringford to serve the village. The disused line now forms a footpath along beside the small River Yar to Newchurch. From its beginning one can look across to Haseley: in the intervening field must have stood the mill, with a pond to drive it taken off the stream, a very rambly waterway but here straightened out for a stretch by the engineers who built the railway line. Arreton has a fine network of footpaths, some leading up on to the down with wide views across to Culver Cliffs and Sandown Bay: others wander off through fields toward Godshill. The riverside path leads through luxuriant banks of water-loving plants such as comfrey and yellow iris.

This south-eastern end of Arreton is the most changed by the twentieth century, for agriculture has largely given way to horticulture and acres of glasshouses wink back in the sun: from the downs they are often mistaken for lakes. The change is even more marked as Arreton merges with Newchurch.

Two pub signs give clues to the sporting nature of Yar valley folk. For hundreds of years there were no foxes on the island, so the hare was much hunted. When Sir Edward Horsey was at Haseley, he would give a lamb in exchange for a live hare brought over from the mainland to increase the local hunting stock. In the eighteenth century, Squire Thatcher kept up the tradition, running a well-known pack of hounds from Wacklands Farm, near Newchurch, where the pub sign shows a pointer, the dog used not to hunt game but to point towards it.

There are various stories accounting for the fox's arrival. One tradition tells how Squire Thatcher's son secretly brought eight cubs over from the Portsmouth area and let them go in the dark. (Percy Stone tells the story in one of his racy ballads.) Next hunting day the pack scented a fox and were off.

Says Squire, "I've run a fair sight
O hares and no run would I miss,
We'm got stoutish hares in the Wight
But I never seed ar'one like this."

The pub on Hale Common, the Fighting Cocks, reveals the Squire's other obsession: he kept some fifty birds in special pens at the farm and was famed as the island's champion breeder. It is said that his birds were even sent to London to fight in an all-England team.

Along Newchurch's main street lie thatched cottages, new bungalows and a Post Office inside a bower of wistaria, but its focus is the church with its unusual wooden tower surmounted by a small spire. Beside it the road suddenly plunges downhill to the valley of the Yar.

At the time of the Domesday survey there seems to have been no manor called Newchurch, which adds strength to the tradition that an older, Saxon church stood here, the "New" one being built by the Normans. Other Domesday names are still familiar though, many as present-day farms—there were Knighton, Branston, Winston, Bathingbourne, Apse and Wroxall, only this last having become a village in its own right. Though there is a fine manor house at Apse, it is some way from the present village.

Knighton was the manor most important to the history of Newchurch. In the Domesday survey, the king held Knighton and the Down, while eight freemen held ploughland and a share of the mill, which was on the site of the present waterworks, down in the valley close under the steep flank of the Down. The house called Knighton stood close by on a mound though now only the stone gateposts remain. By the twelfth century it was owned by the de Morvilles, Hugh de Morville being one of the murderers of Thomas à Becket in Canterbury Cathedral. His son John built the north transept of the church as a kind of expiation, and left money for Mass to be said for his father's soul.

By marriage the manor descended to the de Gorges, then the impecunious Dillingtons. "The de Gorges lived there very well: they had their chapel and there weare many of them buryed and had fayr monuments, ye chapel now is turned to a brewhouse and ye churchyard to an orchard," wrote Sir John Oglander.

Later General Maurice Bocland, M.P. for Yarmouth, owned Knighton, entertaining such celebrities as John Wilkes, Sir Joshua Reynolds and Garrick, the actor.

The village church was founded by Fitz Osborn, enlarged by the monks of Lyra and Beaulieu who painted its walls and raised the tower, but in Cromwell's time the walls were plastered over and the paintings lost: in turn a nineteenth-century restoration tore down a plaster ceiling to reveal the old roof timbers.

On entering this very old and beautifully spacious church, a soaring chancel arch at once draws the eye, but there is much else of interest. The de Morville chapel was taken over by the Dillingtons and is now the vestry, floored by Dillington memorial stones: hanging on the wall is a recently completed family tree of the Dillingtons showing their connections with various other well-known island families, such as the Oglanders of Nunwell, while the Thatchers of Wacklands have several tablets on the nave wall.

The lectern has often been called a pelican, since the brass bird is surrounded by its young and pecking its own breast as that bird is reputed to do, but examine the beak and it becomes clear the bird is the more traditional eagle. It was brought from Frome in Somerset. One of the doors on the north side is blocked up: tradition tells that this was the side from which the devil entered the church, so it was safer not to provide a door.

There is a lovely fourteenth-century rose window deep sunk high on the west wall, and a delightful modern window too. A memorial to Francis Bamford, vicar till 1934, it shows St Francis standing in an Italianate formal garden, delicately gemmed with bright flowers, with a docile wolf and a friendly rabbit.

Much of the churchyard has been cleared, though a sundial from Knighton remains and must be visited, for the churchyard stands on a high terrace with a splendid view, from the downs above Shorwell in the west, across a green pastoral landscape sheltered by hills to the far dramatic plunge of Culver Cliff into Sandown Bay.

Old documents bring vividly to life an older village. A Coroner's Roll for 1377 describes an "inquest on John Grontate. Dispute between John Aleyn and John Grontate in the field called Fenycombe. Grontate took a staff and hit Aleyn so that he fell to the ground wishing to kill him. To save his life, Aleyn took a knife; in the struggle Grontate fell upon that knife and received a wound from which he later died". Fenycombe is the origin of the name Veniscombe, now applied to a house in the village street.

At the Dissolution of Quarr Abbey by Henry VIII, its abbot was appointed vicar of Newchurch. In 1703 there happened a very tempestuous wind which blew down a great many trees and houses. In 1714 William Calloway was paid fifteen shillings for ringing the bells when King George came to England to be crowned. An amazing Church Register entry for 1740 reads, "Dr.

Benson, Bishop of Gloucester confirmed at this parish of Newchurch, five hundred and fifty one persons, of which three hundred who lived in this parish." (The total of island candidates was 1,680.)

A few years later William Bowles of Langbridge left five hundred pounds to purchase land and to build there a school, "that so many boys of poor farmers, labourers and craftsmen of the said village should be taught to read and write". Langbridge is a fine old farmhouse down on the Yar level and opposite to it is the turning called Old School Lane. The house itself, once providing a schoolroom and home for the master, is now divided into two with a modernized front, but the stone, three-storeyed end walls are little changed.

In 1775 poor William Cook died by drinking drams at Farmer John White's wedding. Soon bounty for militia men, raising of Volunteer Bands trained on Soldiering Ground and mention of the village cannon indicate war with France. Churchwardens' accounts for 1781 record also peaceful music in church, ten and sixpence as a present for The Brading Singers, eight shillings for new reeds for the bassoon and hautboy, which were played in the now demolished gallery.

Another entry shows the enormous extent of Newchurch parish—it stretched from the Solent to the Channel, which partly accounts for the amazing number confirmed. It included Ryde and so was responsible for the burial of sixty-eight seamen, drowned in the tragic sudden sinking of the *Royal George*, at a cost of thirteen guineas.

More frivolously, the children used to go round on Shrove Tuesday begging for food to make a last feast before the austerities of Lent closed in:

A-shrovin, a-shrovin, we be come a-shrovin.
Nice meat in a pie, my mouth be very dry,
I wish 'e was as well a wet
I'd sing the louder for a nut.

Certainly climbing the steep hill from river back to village street could make anyone dry—it is called a shute, a common island word for such a gradient. At its foot the bridge no longer appears "lang" because again the Yar has been canalized to fit the railway once running beside it. Upstream a straggle of willows marks the river line, dragonflies flash among reeds, marsh valerian and marguerites; moorhens scuttle for cover; the water meadows where Friesians graze are rich in bird life, a favourite haunt of lapwing, a-flicker with martins and swallows in summer, while the banks are coverts for pheasants and partridges. Downstream, a small weir splashes into a pool.

Beyond the water meadows, market gardens begin again, a traditional way of life here. A hundred years ago there were nine scattered round the village. Several have become nurseries, retailing garden plants and shrubs; the latest trend, to keep down labour costs, is "self picking". In season you can pick your own strawberries, broad beans, cauliflower, deliciously fresh at much reduced prices. Another market garden specializes in sweetcorn, asparagus and garlic.

As you would expect with such soil, Newchurch has gardening clubs, but it also runs a local history society, an art group and a male voice choir, together with a barn dance every month. The controversial scheme to build a new village in the nearby hamlet of Winford will obviously bring a larger population to the area, less native and rooted, more likely to commute to Ryde, Newport or Sandown for work and even play.

Even so there are still walks through gentle unspoilt country, through the oaks of Borthwood Copse perhaps, or to Queens Bower.

But which queen's bower? Tradition places a hunting-lodge here built for a royal lady; some suggest Queen Anne, others Queen Eleanor who was said to be confined in Quarr Abbey and later buried nearby in a golden coffin. But the strongest theory points to Isabella de Fortibus, Lady of the Isle of Wight from 1262 to 1293, one of the wealthiest women in the land, responsible for much building at her residence, Carisbrooke Castle, and known, at least locally, as the Queen of the island, so most likely she it was who rode out over the Newchurch lands with a hawk upon her wrist.

Paths along the Yar lead towards the hamlet of Alverstone. Though the old mill has gone, there are delightful walks by the stream or through the marshes to Sandown. Alverstone has always been famous among lovers of wild flowers for the wealth of water-loving plants. The Isle of Wight Tourist Board publishes a leaflet of nature trails including one here. In high summer marsh willow-herb grows head high, with comfrey in every shade from cream to deepest purple, while moorhens scoot about in the shade of alders and willows; and those ancient plants, the horsetails, thrive on the marshy banks.

The Yar winds on round the back of Sandown to Brading. It must be made plain at once that Brading is a town, the "King's Town" in fact, but in atmosphere it is far closer to St Helens or Niton than to urban streets of Sandown or Ryde: its inclusion is meant as a compliment rather than an insult to its status, for its rich history has affected the whole island.

Today, Brading is a long narrow street of cottages winding downhill then up again to the church: one is called The Barn which has tea gardens behind it and behind them fields stretch away to the east, but to understand the story of Brading one has to remember that the waters of the harbour originally lapped all along the back of these cottages. Like Newport and Newtown, Brading grew up at the head of a deep-water creek or river: this gave it the advantage of a sheltered harbour.

The Roman invasion of the island is thought to have been unopposed. One of the best villas they left behind is in the Morton area of Brading, under the downs. This is open to the public and includes some fascinating mosaic floors. Built in the second century A.D. and occupied for some two hundred years, it appears to have been the centre of a farm estate which pastured sheep on the downs while growing cereals on the lower slopes. Part of the villa complex was a barn, with a corn-drying oven.

After the Romans came Jutish invaders: from place-name evidence it seems they settled most thickly here, along the Yar. In 686, Cadwalla of Wessex conquered the island and later gave this eastern part to one Wulfhere, King of Mercia, who built the town of Woolverton, now lying beneath the trees of St Urian's Copse, then Wilfred converted the people of the island, beginning his first sermon, says tradition, on the hillock now occupied by Brading church, which can thus claim to be the oldest religious foundation on the island, whose entire population in the eighth century was reckoned as twelve hundred families.

After the Danish raids repulsed by King Alfred's navy, the next great event was the Norman Conquest, for William Fitz Osborn, the Norman given responsibility for the island, in turn granted an estate at Brading to Hugh de Oglandre who built the first

Nunwell House. The last Oglander left Nunwell only in 1980.

Brading's crest is enclosed in the words "Ye Kinges Towne", traditionally King Alfred's. Its first charter dated Edward VI refers back to even earlier ones. At one time it returned two members to parliament. Each of them had to be paid fourpence per day and this was found to be so burdensome that the inhabitants petitioned to be disenfranchised. A corn market was held every Monday and a three-day fair, originally held round the Town Hall, but moved up to the downs where "there was more room for junketing", twice a year.

Brading possesses a priceless collection of local documents which add strange footnotes to history. A seventeenth-century map shows a mere group of cottages at the head of Brading Haven, a port for small vessels carrying mostly corn and coal, while cockles and oysters were harvested from the harbour. The parish register for 1677 records the death of "Jowler Knight of Merton, who, rather than he could be charitable to himself, lived like a miserable wretch on ye public charity. He lived in a perpetual slavery through fear and suspicion and perished both his back and belly to fill ye purse". One of the parish books is chillingly entitled "First class, or ordinary poor paupers".

The parish of course owned a gun for its defence: this was inscribed "John and Robert Owine made this pese 1549". Since the down was the traditional place for jollifications, when news of the passing of the Reform Bill reached Brading in 1832, it was dragged up the steep slope to be fired from the summit—but burst! By this time Brading was a flourishing town with its busy harbour and quays, while Ryde was a mere fishing village, but another parish entry shows what could happen to the poor.

Dated 1830, it reports a meeting held to consider "the unjustifiable and unwarrantable measure in contemplation of the Directors and Guardians of the Poor to give premiums to certain persons who will take a number of poor boys and girls with the avowed intention of transporting them to different parts of America, for no other crime than having been born poor. We do most solemnly protest . . ."

The coming of the railway and its embankment finally cut Brading off from the sea, while providing it with a new means of transport: today it is the only village-size place to retain its station and has become much involved in the tourist trade though more for day trips than for accommodation. There is much to see, though the traffic from Ryde to Sandown thunders constantly along the High Street.

Beginning at the Sandown end, one might visit Morton Manor, part of which has recently been opened to the public. The land known as Morton at one time supported two farms and formed part of the estate of the de Aula family who were evidently powerful in these parts as there is a de Aula chapel in Brading church. Later Morton belonged to Yaverland Manor, then to Nunwell. The oldest part of the present house dates from 1526, though rebuilt and enlarged in 1680. Some cracked flagstones lead down to the thirteenth-century remains of the original farm-house. The decor is now largely Georgian with moulded plaster ceilings and symmetrically placed doors—even if they did not lead anywhere. Most of the house is a private family home.

Outside there is a small granary perched on its original staddle-stones, a coach-house and duck pond: future plans include establishing a small vineyard. Close by stands the Roman villa.

The Mall with some elegant Victorian houses leads to a round-about at the end of the High Street and on a bollard in the middle still stands the massive iron ring to which unfortunate bulls were fastened, to be baited. Sir John Oglander says, "It was the custom from time immemorial for the Governor of the Isle of Wight to give five guineas to buy a bull to be baited and given to the poor. The mayor and corporation attended at the bullring in their regalia . . . and a dog, called the Mayor's Dog, ornamented with ribbons, was set at the bull."

Along the High Street terraces of cottages open straight on to the pavement. The terrace pattern was very important in the last century as often the attic of one cottage had access to the one next door. It is said that on the east side of the street, smugglers' escape routes ran right from one end to the other, so that a smuggler pursued into a cottage near the church could well emerge at the Bull Ring, the far end of the village!

Brading is a delightful place for cottage hunting—there are wavy roofs dating back to Queen Elizabeth I, The Russells dated 1790, Georgian with added Victorian bay windows, many from the last century, a few thatched, all prosperous looking without being tarted up for the tourist: a few of them are souvenir or antique shops. The street is particularly charming after dark:

having climbed the hill towards the church one is suddenly face to face with St Wilfred, his saintly face looking down upon the rough heathen at his feet, for this is the tableau currently in the window of Brading Wax Museum. (One theory states the islanders were converted at pain of death . . .) This corner house claims to be the oldest on the island with Roman foundations, later becoming a rectory, then a pub. When alterations were being made, the bones were found of one Louis de Rochefort, a French messenger, murdered in 1646 with the cry upon his lips that he would haunt that house until his bones were returned to France. The present owner took the bones over to Rochefort but could find no trace of Louis' family, so his skeleton still lies confined in the Wax Museum and a tall thin figure is said to glide about the galleries by night.

Opposite stands the old Town Hall, part of its ground floor enclosed only by iron bars. Inside, tucked under the stairs is a cell which was the town gaol, a whipping post and the stocks. The upstairs is often used to exhibit the archives of Brading, old prints, maps and letters, with various original church registers together with period clothes and domestic tools. (There is a newer Town Hall up by the Bull Ring.)

St Wilfred's converts must surely have raised a church upon that famous knoll: it would have been built of wood and so left no trace, but a fine church stands there today, dating from the twelfth century. Its tower at once catches the eye for its lowest storey stands upon pillars so that one enters the church through it, beside rugged wooden steps leading up to the belfry. Founded by the de Insula family, its north chapel was added by the de Aulas (later Hawles) and bears two massive stone tombs, but is at present being restored. The south or Oglander chapel has a rich collection of family tombs, several bearing unusual painted wooden effigies.

The oldest memorial, an incised slab once inlaid with metal, lies by the altar and commemorates John Cherowin, Constable of Portchester Castle 1441. Amongst a wealth of nineteenth-century stained glass, there are the Shepherds at Bethlehem, Christ in the Temple and the story of the prodigal son. Old prints show a gallery and organ over the west entrance, but these have been removed: an archway into the belfry from the church allows a view of another stained-glass window so that on a sunny evening the centre aisle is lit up with long jewel-coloured beams.

Other old drawings show cottages between the tower and the road. On the other side, two other old cottages have been put together in a venture begun in 1974 and now world famous. In 1960, ten-year-old Katherine Munday reviewed her collection of dolls in national costume and decided it was incomplete without a doll from Russia. None was to be found locally, so she wrote to Mr Khrushchev, at the Kremlin, Moscow, and asked him for one—the family regarded it as a joke. But four months later there arrived a Matreshka, a painted wooden doll with others nestled inside. Via school and the local paper, Matreshka reached world Press and television: soon Katherine was inundated with a flood of dolls from dozens of foreign countries, the foundation of a collection finally presented to the public in the Lilliput Doll Museum.

No one need fear pretty-pretty rows of dull china faces. The oldest doll, made of sandstone, dates from 2000 B.C. and came from an Egyptian tomb. Character dolls include Noël Coward, Hitler, a bookie's runner and a witch made of crab's claws. Tiny china dolls, called Frozen Charlottes, used to be put in Christmas puddings. One elegant girl is dressed in material from Queen Caroline's wedding gown. Pedlar dolls, fashioned from chicken skin, were made near Portsmouth in the 1820s, each matchbox-size selling tray set out with tiny fans and strings of beads. There are of course the grand, pretty dolls, particularly those made by Jumeau a hundred years ago, each with a complete change of wardrobe including handbag, jewels and muff—the variety is endless. Nearly every doll has come from its owner and so brings its own story.

One of the most moving is a rag-doll in Polish national costume. She was made, secretly, in a German concentration camp, the only token of gratitude the maker could give to the doctor who saved her life when the camp was liberated.

Lilliput has been such a success that doll specialists come from all over the world. It has branched out into a dolls' hospital and specialist dolls' shop: in 1981 a new wing of the museum was opened.

A little out of the village, under the wooded slope of Brading Down, lies Nunwell House, home until 1980 of the Oglanders who played so large a part in the life of the village. Sir John, that ardent Royalist who entertained Charles I, was devoted to his home. "I have been so foolish as to bestow more money than a wise man would have done in flowers for the garden. It was my content, wearied with study, to solace myself and see the sports of Nature. I planted above a hundred young elms and ashes, some chestnuts and service berries in the grove of my house. When I came to Nunwell I found not one quince tree, when I set at least a thousand."

A later Oglander, William, held a very different point of view. During the Napoleonic Wars, oak for warships fetched high prices: William received one hundred thousand pounds for timber from the estate. In the 1970s the house was at times open to the public while remaining the family home. The new owners reopened it as a holiday attraction with various craftsmen who could be watched at work, and jousting in the grounds. But this was not a financial success and Nunwell closed. So a large question mark now hangs over its future.

Brading makes a good walking centre. A lovely walk for a hot day is along the bottom of the down above Nunwell, through the hanging woods. Whatever William did for the oaks, the beeches remain, huge old trees climbing right up the steep slope with a few chestnuts, sycamores and dark yews. Paths join up with two of the island's long-distance trails, Nunwell, from Sandown to Ryde, and Bembridge, from there to Newport.

By contrast, walks eastwards from the village lead out over the flat green reclaimed lands to the coast and the foot of Culver Down; some circle back to the vicinity of the Anglers Inn, once a sailors' and smugglers' pub at the harbourside, though it had to compete with eight others in the High Street. Now its terrace overlooks the narrow Yar winding through lush fields. The old name, Brading, is said to mean "a broad meadow".

4

Medina Country

Newport stretches northwards, past the prisons at Parkhurst, towards Cowes: Cowes and Gurnard throw red-brick tentacles southwards towards Newport and half-way between, on a plateau above the River Medina, sprawls Northwood. Strung along a busy road, modern houses alternate with service stations and small facories while there in the middle a vast open space is taken up by Plessey Radar. All over the grass huge discs and bowls move slowly round or slide to and fro, being tested.

It would be easy to view Northwood as a mere dormitory suburb of Cowes which, together with East Cowes across the river, is the most industrial part of the island, but this is not so. In fact Cowes was carved out of Northwood Parish in 1894, and to be fair, behind the ribbon development along every road, green fields still stretch away, eastwards to the Medina and south-west to Parkhurst Forest, of which this was, long ago, the North Wood.

Early man has left traces all over the area, mesolithic hearths and flint knives down by the river, a Bronze Age chipping floor or workshop in Ruffins Copse, while other Bronze Age flints and axes have frequently been turned up by the plough. Ruffins is perhaps Roghelonde where a beacon fire was sited in the fourteenth century.

Old Northwood, easily missed, lies down a track on the east of the busy main road. At once red brick is left behind, fields stretch away on either side and soon there appears a farm, the church with old houses and cottages close about it, all compact and tranquil. (Beneath the fields lie traces of still older cottages.) In the twelfth century, the forest stretched right across the north of the island and all this land belonged to the parish of Carisbrooke, though the church was miles away through wild woodland. So a chapel to Carisbrooke was built here to serve those in the northern part of the parish, though till the end of the fifteenth century the dead had to be taken to Carisbrooke for burial. In 1512 some land was conveyed to the Brothers and Sisters of St John the Baptist, who had built a religious house near the church, later known as the Church House. This was short-lived, being suppressed by Henry VIII in 1536, though the house was still standing in 1690 and an old barn, inscribed "restored 1742", which may have been the Brothers' grange, survived till 1901. Nothing remains of the foundation now, though the north doorway of the church may have originated there.

Old farm buildings lean against the churchyard wall: the church itself with mellow tiled roof and slender spire is bowered among huge old chestnuts, sycamores and dark yews. An old print shows the church with a tower, an extraordinary squat erection, looking like a wooden box lowered on to the roof: the spire was erected in 1864, made of oak thrown out from Carisbrooke church during its Victorian restoration.

Chawton Farm, beside the churchyard, is mentioned as early as 1248 when it was called Caulkstone and would have been a clearing in the forest, like Medham to the north, which belonged to William de Medeme in 1299.

Several rectors of Northwood had the amiable habit of jotting down not only local news but how to foretell the weather and the tithe rules in their registers. In 1722 Northwood church is found "in worse repair than I can express", by its new vicar Dr

Troughear. The vicar was entitled to a tithe, or tenth, from his parishioners. "If any man take to pasture any ews of any dwelling out of this parish, lambs of them shall be tithed together. What is of Ten, they pay One. Of geese they pay the tenth and of Seven they pay One and take three farthings. For eggs, apples, pears, onions and garlic they pay the tenth. Hempseed they pay none."

An entry for 1735 shows a new development in the island industry of salt making; at that time of course the parish included all the northern seaboard of Cowes. "Tythe of salt for the first three years, two and sixpence per annum, for the four following years, five shillings per annum so long as the said Thomas Troughear do live. N.B. I accepted of so small a composition for my own time because this Mr Day's saltern were the first in this parish—my successor may very well insist upon ten shillings per pan."

Though the main industry of shipbuilding became concentrated at Cowes, there was a prosperous shipyard higher up the river at Hurstake in the eighteenth century, and oyster beds flourished in the estuary. Later came the railway, the line from Cowes to Newport running along the river bank: though there was no Northwood station, trains could stop at Medina Cement Works.

However, the "growth industry" of the nineteenth century was brick and tile making, dominated by the Pritchett family who came to the island in 1798 to make rebate tiles for the first Parkhurst Barracks. Later Edmund Pritchett established a brick-works at Shamblers, near the river. When the government decreed that land must be properly drained, the Ward estate, which reputedly stretched from Cowes to Freshwater at that time, asked Edmund to advise them on setting up a works to make land drain-pipes. Edmund built the works at Hillis, astutely putting in his son William as manager. After sufficient pipes had been made, the kilns were turned over to bricks and tiles. A horse operated a mill where local clay was prepared, while the bricks were dried by sun and wind.

But the Pritchetts were not slow in taking up new machinery: soon they were exporting flower pots to the Channel Islands and had the honour of supplying garden pottery for the grounds of Queen Victoria's new mansion at Osborne. To keep up with demand, other brick works were opened in Northwood, including one at Oxford Street.

It is many years now since a single brick was made on the island: for years the Hillis site lay derelict, the kilns crumbling away under brambles. Then the site was taken over by a marine engineering firm, one of the five kilns has been repaired and is now once again producing pottery.

The history of the Ward family belongs properly to Cowes, where the great mansion they built, Northwood House, is still a focal point amid its parkland, but their washing was done in Northwood village. A picturesque old house in Pallance Road, now called Rose Cottage, was the laundry and it still possesses a very long narrow garden which was the drying ground.

In this century, industry tends to spread here from Cowes rather than grow from the terrain. During the 1914 war when the big shipbuilding firm of J. S. White and Co. down on the Medina estuary were also turning out aircraft, they bought a vast field at Northwood, built hangars and a factory and used the rest as an airfield. New bombers took off for their first airfields while sea-planes were rolled down to the river on trolleys. Today factories make lampshades and industrial engines.

So Northwood is a curious mix, for behind the dormitory-suburb semis and bungalows, between the garages and factories, still spread the green fields of farms that were once clearings in the forest. As if to remind one of their continuing importance, one of these fields is the permanent site of the all-island agricultural show, held at the end of July.

This is a real show-case for rural Wight; all day two show rings are busy with riding events, packs of beagles and foxhounds, sheepdog trials, vintage steam engines and, most important, the grand parade of prize-winning cattle and horses. Will Shate Farm, Brighstone, win again, with their Jersey herd which has the oldest pedigree in Britain? Will Dean Farm, Whitwell, get the cup for their well-known Dorset Horn sheep? Friesians are the commonest cattle on the island.

Some of the large circle of stands are taken by mainland firms but the rest show the extraordinary variety of island enterprises, shipbuilding, gipsy caravans, bird fanciers, dog training, clay pigeon shooting, lace making, Sea Scouts, rabbit clubs, light opera, with of course marquees full of flowers, and Women's Institute stalls.

Just up the road stands the Horseshoe Inn, so named because

the wheelwright's and forge used to stand next door. The pub does a variety of meals, from hot ones with chips to ploughman's lunches, and has a very pleasant lounge decorated with models of shire horses, wagon wheels and nail-head pictures of horses, but its greatest curiosity is the well. This was discovered when the pub was extended northwards over the old garden: now the lounge floor has a glass lid in the middle: when the light is on beneath it, customers can watch goldfish swimming about far below: there were carp too at one time, but they mysteriously disappeared after a heavy rain storm.

Along the direct road to Cowes stands an old cottage sensitively modernized, with the words Flower Pot painted large above the front door. This was once another pub. Along Pallance Road to the west stands the Travellers Joy which sells real ale: this was recently closed down by the brewers who own it, but such was the force of public outcry and the flood of indignant letters to local papers, it has now been reopened. Although in this case it may well refer to the beer, "travellers joy" is an island name for the wild cream-flowered clematis, before it goes to seed and becomes "old man's beard".

Though the river is only three quarters of a mile from the Horseshoe on the main road, it seems to impinge little on the life of Northwood. The old railway line from Newport to Cowes is now a riverside path and a track is signposted to join up with it. Beyond banks of willow-herb, cow parsley or St John's wort in their season, lie fields—of sheep on one side, goats and geese on the other—while ahead, inviting woods hide the river. But, at the time of writing, the stile is blocked up, the Medina unreachable.

There are a few other field paths, but the best walking is to be found at the southern boundaries of the village, where the forest now begins, at Noke Common and Marks Corner.

Older inhabitants of Marks Corner can still remember the Saturday donkey parades when the laundry women would set off, each driving her cart full of clean linen and wearing a large straw hat, to deliver to the "posh" houses in Cowes and collect the next week's washing: often a local boy would be taken along to mind the donkey while house calls were made, his wage a bag of bull's-eyes. A larger cart, pulled by three donkeys, took fruit and vegetables including strawberries from the strawberry field, to the Cowes gentry.

Though the forest gates were normally locked against wheeled traffic, some of those gentry, whose firms made yachts for the royal family, were given special permission to drive in the forest, which is Crown land. On the other hand, the locals grew up used to walking, for that was how the children reached Northwood School; they had to go along Slovens Hall—a lane, over Paint Hill, down Dirty Lane, over Pallance Brook and up Long Ground.

During the 1914 war, charcoal was made in the forest since it was needed for the making of gunpowder. Two foresters would camp out for a week at a time under a cart sheet, keeping a slow fire burning under a roof of turves, taking turns to keep watch at night as the wood must never be allowed enough air for it to burst into flame. A minor use of charcoal locally was to purify rainwater for drinking since many cottages had only the water that ran off their own roofs.

During the last week in May and the first in June, women worked in the forest, stripping bark from felled oaks and sacking it up for the tanneries in Newport and Carisbrooke.

When an old cottage on the forest side of Northwood was pulled down, it was found to have been built of clay and strengthened with chopped up furze bushes, and the drains consisted of trenches, dug out, filled with a thick layer of oak leaves and then earth was thrown back on the top. This appeared to have worked most efficiently as a soak-away for many years.

On the opposite side to the forest, Northwood merges into Gurnard. On old maps the name appears as Gurnet, the name of a large-headed sea fish with mailed cheeks which today survives on the badge of Gurnard sailing club. The centre of the village round which stand the church, pub and a few shops is largely Victorian or later with an outer rim of modern suburban estates, for the oldest records are connected with the shore, half a mile downhill whichever of several roads one takes.

One of the eight known Roman villas was situated on the shore of Gurnard marsh: excavated in 1864 it has long since disappeared under the waves, which is particularly tantalizing since it is the only one by the sea. Was it a fort built against raiding Saxons, or a trading post perhaps? A theory was current at one time that tin from Cornwall was sent up to Lepe in Hampshire, over the Solent to Gurnard and across the island along a straight road beginning at Rew Street to Puckaster Cove, for export to

Rome, a variant being that the tin was driven in carts from Lepe to Gurnard across a causeway.

Certainly Gurnard was an important landing place long before Cowes. Even in the seventeenth century one reads, "My Lord Conway, Captain of the Isle of Wight came into our island 14th September 1627, having been Captain thereof two years and never seen it. He landed at Gurnard where all the gentlemen met him and brought him to the castle." Later came an even more important guest, to stay with the Captain of the island at Yarmouth. "In 1671 Charles II landed at Gurnard Bay and passed through Parkhurst Forest (by a road constructed at the express direction of Sir Robert Holmes)."

Today the marsh is covered with summer beach chalets and cafés, but older inhabitants can remember when the only building was Cooks Cottage, on the estuary of the little stream called The Luck. The lane across was gated at each end and the marsh used for grazing cattle, though the army camped near the cottage in the 1914 war to guard the telephone cable from the mainland which came ashore there. At that time the ridge where the chalets nearest to the sea now stand, formed the inner run of a large lagoon, since eroded away. Once a year Arnold's used to set up their fairground on the land between lane and sea. The first chalets appeared in the 1920s.

Cockleton Lane leads down to the west end of the marsh: a great part of its length was once occupied by The Dell and its grounds. These were thrown open to the children of Gurnard village every Good Friday so that they might pick primroses to decorate the church for Easter; later in the summer they were invited again for a Strawberry Feast. The house is gone now, its grounds taken up by Gurnard Pines Holiday Camp, a pleasantly spacious and wooded site well tucked away.

Half-way up from the marsh stood a coastguard's station: today it is a row of private houses at right angles to the road, the largest, now called Wheel House, was for the chief coastguard. Down on the beach below stand a double row of black piles, the ruins of the coastguard jetty. The beach tends to be narrow, soon becoming a jumble of dark seaweedy rocks.

Further east the beach is sandier: here stands a row of beach huts backed by a small wood and a green sloping down to another stream called the Jordan. Before the new road opened up this beach, the wood stretched much further and was known for wild daffodils and bee orchids.

The oldest buildings in inland Gurnard tend to be in the lower village, round the back of the marsh where a few stone or thatched cottages remain. Along Rew Street stands a beautiful old cart shed with its original timbers. Another which takes the eye is the "Round House" or toll-gate cottage at the top of Tutton's Hill. Otherwise, the older buildings are Victorian, many built with bricks produced once more by the Pritchett family.

In 1850 Edmund Pritchett, who had the brickyard at Shamblers, learned that a new estate was to be put up at Gurnard. He bought the first building plot and built a kiln—this became the Elim Brickyard. Some of its output was "white bricks", actually a pale yellow colour, made with cream-coloured clay from Gurnard cliffs. Edmund had to provide for ten children so it was fortunate he had a good business head. Later he obtained the contract to supply bricks for the building of the forts at Yarmouth and a new yard was opened, called Jordan, close to the sea. From here the bricks were loaded on to boats and sailed round to Yarmouth.

Up by the centre of the village, the small church is built of "white" bricks, with corner decorations of red: otherwise it is a plain building with a bell turret, erected in the 1890s.

The best walks from Gurnard are by the sea. The north-west coast path strikes off across the cliffs from the western end of the marsh, providing fifteen miles of quiet fields, lanes and coast to Yarmouth and Totland: for the less rugged, Princes Parade, a wide pavement along the sea wall, leads from the Woodvale beach all the way into Cowes.

This road and walk are the result of a job creation scheme in the slump years of the mid 1920s (formerly only a muddy path led along the top of the shore). It was opened by the Prince of Wales in 1926 and has been a favourite road for islanders ever since. Of course for big events like the Power Boat Race, the start of the Fastnett and all of Cowes Week it is crowded from end to end, but even in winter there are always people about, for the Solent is busy all the year round with ferries, hovercraft on trials from East Cowes, nippy little hydrofoils whipping over to Southampton in twenty minutes, huge container ships stacked high, tankers waiting to go up to the Fawley Refinery, the *Q.E.2*, or someone practising for the annual tin-bath race, yachts of every size and coasters heading for the River Medina.

Across a plateau on the eastern side of the river lies the scattered village of Whippingham, a green and rural scene in contrast to Northwood and Gurnard, with one fairly busy main road leading to the ferry terminal and East Cowes and a few well-scattered areas of new building.

The name is perhaps derived from "the homestead of Wippa, a Jute". The parish at one time included all the eastern bank of the Medina from the Solent to Newport, but in 1894 East Cowes was taken out of it. For hundreds of years it was a place of scattered farms, with a secluded manor house, and a church and pub down by the river: in 1800 the population was eight hundred. All that was altered by the coming of Queen Victoria.

The name Osborne was originally East Bourne, which became Austerburne, and so merely means east of the river. The estate once belonged to the Bowerman family who will be met again at Brooke, but was bought in the seventeenth century by Eustace Mann. During the Civil War, he became worried about his wealth, should battle extend to the island so, according to Adam's history, "he sagely buried a large sum of gold and silver in the wood on his estate and as sagely omitted to distinguish the spot by any private mark, so that when more peaceful times ensued, he was unable to recover his concealed treasures". After the Restoration of Charles II, he took care to obtain from the crown a grant "of all waifs, strays and treasure trove, with right of warren", but the treasure was never found and the land ever after called Money Coppice.

Nevertheless his son John set up a charity to look after orphan children of East Cowes and Whippingham. His daughter married a Blachford, the family who built the original Osborne House in the eighteenth century, described as "one of the best chosen residences on the island, on a fine spacious lawn that leads to the sea".

Princess Victoria fell in love with the Isle of Wight when she stayed at Norris Castle, near East Cowes, as a girl: after her accession and marriage she tried to buy the castle and being thwarted of that, bought the next best thing, the house next door, Osborne. The Blachfords' mansion was pulled down, and in its place rose the Italianate palace designed by the Prince Consort and Thomas Cubitt. Finished in 1851, it stood in two thousand acres terracing down to the sea, and is now a great island show-place, visitors coming from all over the world to revel in its royal treasures and beautiful gardens.

The buildings by the Prince of Wales Gate were the Royal Naval College, opened by Edward VII in 1903. Cadets came from school to spend two years at Osborne, then two at Dartmouth before they were sent to sea. The then Prince of Wales and the Duke of York spent two years there. The cadets used to row up to the pub called Folly to buy chocolate. When the college was closed down in 1921, the locals shook their heads darkly and muttered they'd always said the place was damp!

Queen Victoria's hand is still evident: all over Whippingham stand her estate houses, almshouses, even a "new" church, and many stories about her have been handed down in local families. When dances were held for the servants there were strict rules that no couple should dance together more than once: the shoe-maker's daughter could not resist another turn with her boy-friend, so she was never invited again.

But the Queen took a great interest in everyone on the estate. Her most frequent drive round was from Osborne House along Mount Road, down to Kings Quay, then along Alverstone Road, where the royal kennels were, past the blacksmith's shop on the corner and home. Several estate houses had special lavatories reserved for the Queen in case she was taken short en route. If there was sickness in a family, baskets of food would be sent down. The Queen was particularly fond of the Flux family. Mr Flux was head woodman on the estate: the Queen would call in to give toys to his family of four sons. Some families still treasure dolls given to the estate children as Christmas presents: there is one made of porcelain in the Brading museum.

By contrast there seem few memories of the Prince Consort. Of course he died many years before his wife, but he was a man of wide interests and fostered new ideas in agriculture at Barton Farm. His most lasting influence here though, is as part architect of Osborne House, Whippingham church and various other estate houses.

A church at Whippingham is mentioned in the Domesday survey, founded by William Fitz Osborne, and later dedicated to St Mildred, a Saxon princess. This old church was reconstructed by Nash in 1804, but had a short life in its new form. The Prince Consort designed a completely new structure, opened in 1861. No one interested in churches should miss this unique building; it lies among the homely river meadows like some illustration to Hans Andersen, an exotic Rhenish-cum-Gothic castle, the strong square tower capped by five soaring pinnacles. The inside is equally impressive, the central crossing lit by a great octagonal lantern, the transepts by rose windows: the beautiful bronze screen has an unusual design of slender trees. Everywhere are memorials to Victorian royalty.

Amongst all these nineteenth-century riches stands a rugged fragment of carved stone, a reminder of the original church, set in the south porch, while a modern acquisition is the carpet used at Westminster Abbey at the Coronation of Queen Elizabeth II.

In the churchyard are many memorials to royal servants, keepers, bailiffs and maids, including Andrew Toward, "faithful Steward" for twenty-nine years. Opposite stands a striking row of terracotta-coloured almshouses, built for retired servants and recently refurbished.

More recently much of the land here belonged to Padmore House. This was originally a seventeenth-century farmhouse but has been enlarged in Queen Anne style. The seven Miss Jollifes lived there in the last century: they used to entertain Queen Victoria and at other times travelled the locality in a trap drawn by a team of donkeys. Surplus trees and bushes from the large gardens were thrown out on the bank of the river, so there grew up a copse, The Rookery, which was a splendid mixture of cherry and oak, gooseberry, blackberry, plum and hydrangea: at the edge grew early purple orchids and quaking grass which the local children called "kettle cases" and "wiggle waggas".

It was an important day for Whippingham when Padmore was bought by a Mr Saunders, for he was to become half of the great ship and aircraft building firm of Saunders Roe at East Cowes, and a notable benefactor. He built Whippingham village hall, now the school, and had electricity brought to the church, but his scheme to bridge the Medina and build a road along the east bank did not succeed. When Saunders Roe began to build seaplanes, these were tested along the river below Padmore. There was reputedly a secret passage, dating from smuggling days, which led from the house down under the meadows to the Folly Inn, on the Medina shore.

Some three hundred years ago, on an exceptionally high spring tide, a sloop ran aground and was stranded on the river bank. As she could not be floated off, the captain built on a room and settled down there: the first written mention of Folly is in 1725. When a new landlord took over in 1907, there were no glasses, only Toby jugs bearing Queen Victoria's crest, while the trays and teapots were all pewter. On the pear tree outside customers used to play the old country game of Ring the Bull, with a rope and an iron ring. If one of the village horses was sick, it would be brought down and given a gallon of warm ale—a certain cure. Kingfishers would perch in a row on the jetty rail and ducks queue up for the lees of beer barrels tipped out on to the bank, which made them wobbly on their feet.

The pub has been famous for its annual regatta held in September ever since 1913. The programme then included walking the greasy pole, tug of war—married ladies versus single—Eating Treacle Bun Race, with sports and dancing on the green, all kinds of boat races, and the band of Princess Beatrice's Isle of Wight Rifles.

A pub with such a strange history should be haunted and the tales about Folly from past owners are the more impressive for the vagueness of the apparitions. Sometimes a cloud of grey fog would wreath through the rooms and the dogs whine with their coats bristling: at night with everyone in bed, notes would sound on the piano, and on one dark staircase it seemed an arm would lean heavily across your shoulders as if someone needed to be helped up—one room did have a bullet hole in the ceiling.

Today Folly is much modernized. A centre for small-boat enthusiasts it has a restaurant and a terrace with lovely views of the river right up to Newport and the downs beyond.

The river bank, where many small boats are hauled up makes an interesting study in wild flowers—there is sea purslane, sea beet, sea plantain and scurvy grass at first but up river where the tidal influence becomes weaker these gradually die out, their place taken by campions and thickets of dog roses. At low tide wide banks of mud are exposed, rich feeding for ringed plover, dunlin and sandpiper. Often little grebe can be seen diving in the main channel and a flock of black and white oyster-catchers flies urgently past.

During the First World War, factories, extensions of those at East Cowes, were built along the Whippingham water front: even today the river path from Newport comes to an end at the pub, its way north blocked by Folly Works.

The famous yacht designer and builder Uffa Fox went to Whippingham School as a boy, though he lived in East Cowes. In those days the boys learned gardening, while the girls had cookery lessons for which they had to walk into East Cowes, cross the river on the floating bridge and through West Cowes to Denmark Road School—at other times they had to darn the teacher's stockings! Later, Uffa was to buy land by the Rookery Copse (now a caravan site) and build a house there. As its grounds went right down to the water, he was able to have his private floating bridge brought up river and established on his land so that he could convert it into a workshop.

An older resident of Whippingham, whose father taught Uffa to row, remembers how her mother made ready for winter. Eggs were put down in a bucket of isinglass; butter salted; runner beans put in brine; mushrooms, cabbage and onions pickled and the goat mated to be in milk. Father would supplement supplies by catching shrimps, crabs and winkles and growing black winter radishes, and watercress in the stream.

Barton Manor lies away from both river and road in one of the quietest corners of the whole island. It may be overshadowed by the fame of royal Osborne next door, but its history is far older. In 1272 the Rectors of Godshill and Shalfleet founded a religious house here, Barton Oratory, under the Augustinian rule, with an arch-priest in charge, but by 1386 the building was found in a very dilapidated state and the arch-priest suspended. The Oratory came to an end under Henry VI and was given to Winchester College. From its ruins rose Barton Court House, described in the seventeenth century as "very ancient, moated round with a drawbridge and a church now converted to a barn".

When Queen Victoria built Osborne she bought Barton also. Prince Albert had the house gutted and largely rebuilt. During this "restoriation" a secret chapel was found where Mass had been said after it was forbidden at the Reformation, and also one massive section of wall dating right back to the Oratory. Part of the low ground, once the moat, was turned into a skating rink for the Queen and the manor used as a guest house for foreign royalty, including the Empress Frederick of Germany and King Leopold of the Belgians.

Edward VII built the wide terraces of lawn which fall to the lake, then the manor was sold into private hands in 1922. The new owners planted a quarter of a million bulbs round the lake: later the skating rink was turned into a water garden. Now the grounds have been opened to the public and Barton has begun a new era in its long history, as a centre for wine making.

The visitor can view the five-acre vineyard planted in 1977, stroll round the Secret Garden, the lake with thatched boathouse, the water garden where a series of pools lie among brilliant beds of rudbeckias and loosestrife, and a woodland walk. The house itself in grey stone with Tudor-style high gables and chimneys is interesting for its history: the wall to the left of the front door, showing a line of blocked-up lancet windows, is the remains of the Oratory. Queen Victoria's own apartments were in the south-east wing. (What an army of local labour must have been needed to maintain Barton and Osborne.)

A creamery and cottage adjoining the house have been converted into a winery and café. Here stands all the machinery for the making of Barton Manor Medium Dry White Wine: it can be bought by the glass or bottle.

Apart from Osborne House, the Medina villages are not famous for their "beauty spots", like Godshill and Bonchurch, but nevertheless they are well worth exploring.

5

Central Wight

The clock tower on Whitecroft Hospital is probably the nearest landmark to the exact centre of the island, but the tall brick chimney at Rookley used to be pointed out as marking that spot. High on a slope of down, Rookley enjoys wide views eastward across the Vale of Arreton to the downs beyond, though it is not in itself a village of much charm. Large new bungalow estates have added to the red brick strung along a busy main road.

But there are old and interesting houses to be found. The oldest and most attractive part of the village clusters round the road junction, where the nineteenth-century schoolhouse, now elegantly converted as a dwelling, faces a tiny green with flower-beds and seat, set up for the Queen's Jubilee in 1977. Nearby stands Highwood Lodge, now painted white, a handsome three-gabled house reckoned to be midway between Cowes and Ventnor, for here the carriage horses used to be changed, when on that journey. Along the Niton road is the thatched Malt

Queen Victoria's Almshouses, Whippingham

The Folly Inn on the River Medina, Whippingham

The Chequers Inn, near Rookley

Godshill

Park View garden, Wroxall

Dean Farm buildings, Whitwell

The newer St Boniface, Bonchurch

Bonchurch Pond

Gatcombe Valley

Niton cottages

Chale Church

The Green, Chale

House—in fact all through the village, eighteenth- and nineteenth-century cottages alternate with the new.

Rookley Manor, while a pleasant stone house with fretwork barge-boards, is not really the village manor—that is Pidford, a Jacobean house secluded among its trees towards Newport. The manor of Rookley, using the word in its original meaning as an estate of land, is first mentioned in 1203, when Philip of Blackpan was granted pasture rights. The name was originally Roclee, then Roucle, and seems to mean the obvious, a rooky place.

Gravel was dug near the village, and later clay for an early brickworks. Godshill School log-book has an entry for 1866: "July 5. Gave leave for two boys to go for summer months for brick making." But the enterprise which was to transform Rookley began in 1924 when the Pritchett family, after a slump in their fortunes, decided to open a works here on a site in the middle of the village, which contained deposits of clay and suitable sand, besides being central for distribution round the island. They began with a few tools, a shed and one kiln.

Slowly the yard grew. A railway brought up sand and clay from the pits behind. Hand-moulded facing bricks, roof tiles and flower pots were turned out. After the building of a power house, the whole complex throbbed with energy, day and night. New machinery using the semi-dry process meant that a brick could be made in a mere half-hour from pit to kiln: in its heyday the yard could turn out a hundred thousand common bricks a week. By this time its great sprawl of sheds, kilns and stockpiles, with the tall chimney built in 1935, and a constant flow of lorries, dominated the village. To most people the name Rookley *meant* bricks. After buying the white clay deposits at Quarry Lane, Newbridge, the yard made Primrose Facing Bricks: one of its largest orders was to supply half a million for the building of County Hall in Newport.

On another scale, the Pritchetts were gifted craftsmen: many island homes possess their beautifully hand-made jugs, vases or pots, in dark bluish red or primrose-coloured pottery, each individually decorated with thumb or scratch patterns.

The war with its switch of manpower away from building brought an end to this flourishing scene. A few later attempts to revive it came to nothing. For many years the acres lay derelict, with smashed glass, broken machinery and sheer-sided pits—an ugly and dangerous blot on the whole village.

Now at last new life is being born. The site of the actual works has been designated an industrial estate. There is a petrol station, a small factory making kitchen units, and others being built. While this does not add to the beauty of Rookley, at least it brings some employment.

However, the other half of the site, the old clay and sand diggings, are being transformed into a green and pleasant land, as Rookley Country Park. The claypits form a fine lake fringed with bulrushes, their banks turfed and planted with six hundred young trees, many oak and maple, while the sandpits are to be filled in and landscaped. Already the restaurant is finished, together with an assault course, adventure playground and a putting course. There are plans for boating on the lake, a kids' castle, dancing in the restaurant block, the introduction of wild life—Rookley has seen nothing like this before.

The old boundaries of the brickworks site are marked by two handsome nineteen-thirties houses, one at each end, built by the Pritchett family for themselves, with matching terracotta flourishes on the gables.

Above Rookley lies Bleak Down, called La Blakedon in 1190, meaning pale and bare—in fact bleak, but along its flattened ridge lies a habitat rare on the island, acid moorland. Here flourished both the stripey pink flowers of bog pimpernel and the five-foot leaves of royal fern, but alas, the land with its worked out gravel pits has for some years been an official rubbish dump. Perhaps the yellow spires of bog asphodel, or the fly-eating sundew, survive here and there.

However, another walk from Rookley leads down to the valley of the infant River Medina, its banks bright with foxgloves in their season, a botanist's delight where some of the Bleak Down flora still survive, and jewel-coloured dragon-flies and damselflies flit above the stream. Island children were commonly brought up to believe that dragon-flies possessed stings venomous as adders and since they were always found by water, they were reckoned to be guardians of the fish. Children were taught a charm rhyme invoking the insect by its local name:

Snakes stang, snakes stang, flee all about the brooks
And sting all the bad boys that for the fishes looks.

Along the ridge of Bleak Down and alone on its windswept

heath stands the Chequers Inn, an unusual slate-hung pub associated with smuggling. Bleak Down was the main route from Niton and St Lawrence on the coast, but a Customs Officer lived further along at Rookley, so contraband spirit was often slipped down the lane past the pub and, through a circuitous route via Merston, finally reached Newport. Kegs taken direct to Newport were often hidden under a layer of fish, Chale Bay mackerel, for example.

There are various stables and riding establishments on the island, with a particular concentration here in central Wight. Just below the Chequers stands Lake Farm, the only stables with an indoor riding school. Fifty-four horses are accommodated in ranges of new stables and the undulating fields around, with a few more at livery. In the enormous covered school, toddlers try out their first ponies, those already expert learn the finer points of dressage and through the winter shows are held most weekends. There are plans to provide a new gallery and a restaurant.

Rides taken outside do no road work but use the wealth of bridle paths over the downs or down to the river valley. These include pony club rallies, meetings of the Riding for Disabled Club and rides for the mentally handicapped. A few visitors find their way through the narrow lanes but most of the riders who come to Lake Farm are local.

Along the lower road out of Rookley where two lanes make an inconspicuous crossroads, is Bohemia Corner: no one knows why this rural spot should have a name from middle Europe—in any case the locals tend to call it Bo-amy, but Bohemia is important to the whole island as the address of the "Dogs Home", run by the R.S.P.C.A. and opened in 1956, the site being chosen as both central and rural. It consisted then of two cottages and a vast orchard. Most of the apple trees are still there, providing a pleasant shady setting for the kennels and, more important still, a sound barrier round the inevitable barking.

The main work of the home is to house strays brought in by the police, who pay a week's board for each: if they are not claimed after eight days, the Superintendent sets about finding new homes. A fairly steady stream of prospective new owners come to Bohemia Corner. Large dogs such as Dobermanns and mastiffs are the most difficult candidates.

The home also boards dogs whose owners are taken ill. Sometimes dogs are found simply tied to the front gate, and boxes of kittens may arrive in the night, for it should rightly be called The Animal Home now. A cattery was added in 1965, but other boarders include guinea pigs, swans, a vicious ferret and a goat recovering from an attack by a bull terrier. There would be many more bird casualties if these were not treated elsewhere.

One important, if little publicized, new development is the setting up of special isolation kennels in case of rabies. The island is totally vulnerable to the landing of small boats from the continent and the exercising of dogs which may have been exposed to this hideous disease: it is simply not possible to watch all the little creeks and inlets, especially at night.

But the everyday face of Bohemia is the happier one of care for the *un*wanted, and new owners coming away with a dog who really *is* wanted once more. Some two hundred found new homes last year.

From Bohemia Corner the road winds on through green farmlands to Godshill, a pretty village full of quaint corners and thatched cottages, its history deeply interwoven with the story of the "big house", Appuldurcombe,* whose name means the valley of the apple trees, or pool of water in the hollow.

The first building to bear the name was a priory founded about 1100 as a cell to one in Normandy: at first it flourished, receiving the endowment of Week and exemption from local taxes. The attached farm kept a flock of four hundred sheep, known for their high-quality wool, on the downs above, while herds of pigs roamed the oakwoods. A peaceful life it sounds but was not always so. In 1307 the bishop presented a clerk to the living of Godshill which angered the monks who wished to get their hands on the church revenue. "They entered violently into the church armed with different kinds of weapons and closed the portals, contrary to the canons; and presume sacrilegiously to occupy and fortify the church."

A few years later, the Priory rent was in debt, but pardoned by the king "by reason of the great mortality there", caused by the Black Death. In the next century, when priories belonging to foreign abbeys were closed down, Appuldurcombe became a convent. Later it passed through the Leigh family to its heyday under the Worsleys, who pulled down an Elizabethan house to build a more fashionable one on classic lines.

Sir James Worsley was page to Henry VII and later a favourite of Henry VIII, possessor of various tiles such as "keeper of lions in the Tower of London" and more important, Captain of the Isle of Wight. His son Richard also held this office and received a stern letter from the King abjuring him to stamp out poaching, which began: "Trusty and well beloved we greet you well and being credibly informed that ye Games of Partriche and pheasant is much decayed by the permission and sufferance of such lewd persons as do daily with nets and other engines take the same . . ." The King was obviously looking ahead, for later he paid a visit to Appuldurcombe probably to engage in his favourite sport of hawking.

The last of the Worsley family, Henrietta, married Charles Pelham, later Lord Yarborough. In 1815 he gathered together some friends keen on the fairly new sport of yachting and formed The Yacht Club. Soon even the Prince Regent wished to join: in 1833 this became The Royal Yacht Squadron. Lord Yarborough was famous for his fast craft *Falcon* and so keen to keep in touch with her, that he built a signalling station on the down above Appuldurcombe from which he could communicate with Cowes Roads. Fanny Oglander was rather condescending and wrote in a letter, "Lord Yarborough spent his Christmas at Appuldurconbe and had various parties of the *Natives* at dinner. Lord Yarborough improved the house very much last year, including a new entrance."

There were great junketings held on the estate at the end of a good harvest, with copious healths being drunk and sports held near the signal station. Two teams of cart horses were kept, to fetch supplies from Newport on alternate days.

But later the house declined, though it once more sheltered a community of monks while Quarr Abbey was being built. The grounds of Appuldurcombe are said to be haunted by the ghost of a mad monk ringing a handbell. Today the ruins are cared for by the Ministry of Works and open to the public. Standing in Godshill village the visitor may well ask where Appuldurcombe *is*, for the entrance, quite near the house, is in the centre of Wroxall village: but the original long drive, now a public foot-path, wound from Godshill, through the park and an imposing archway and it is Godshill where the Worsleys are ever present.

Their heraldic beast resembling a griffin and their names abound in village and church.

For example, at the southern end of Godshill stands The Griffin, an imposing stone house with huge Elizabethan-style chimneys, though actually erected by Lord Yarborough and originally thatched. The pub has a special room for children and a spacious garden.

On summer afternoons, the village seethes with visitors, often so thick across the road they actually bring traffic to a halt! They have come to see Ye Olde Godshill, to visit the Toy Museum, the Cider Barn, the Shell Museum, the Witch's Brewery, Lucky Wishing Well, aviary of exotic birds, The Olde Smithy and Forge, the Model Village, or to enjoy cream teas in pretty gardens, or visit the various antique and souvenir shops.

Though one can buy Lucky Horseshoes, Godshill Gnomes tee shirts and tea towels, the shops are splendid bazaars catering for everyone, with lucky Godshill buttons, reproduction Victorian lustre candlesticks at thirty pounds, cactus gardens, elegant tweeds from Welsh and Scottish mills, funny hats, silk scarves from India and of course whole armies of brass Appuldurcombe monks.

Thatch and roses, hanging baskets of bright flowers, quaint lettering, old trees all conspire to make ye olde Godshill an attractive tourist centre with plenty to look at.

In winter the village reverts to its proper self, the centre of a long-established agricultural community. Along the street the cottages can now be seen to be truly old, not just Olde Worlde. Stone Cross Cottage dates from 1600; the fine stone one next to the school bears the Worsley griffin over the front door; at Essex Cottage, Princess Beatrice used to take tea on her drives round the island. There is a new housing estate, grouped round a close off the main road and actually much quieter than the old village which bears a steady stream of traffic even off season.

The village general store puts up a list in its window of current planning applications for the area, together with the Parish Council's recommendation and the planning authority's decision: in the current list there is one hundred per cent agreement between the two bodies concerned. The old school house presents its Victorian stone façade to the street and is still in use with a complex of modern classrooms built on behind it, and a history going back some four hundred years.

In 1520, Sir John Leigh of Appuldurcombe obtained a licence from Henry VIII for part of the parish church to be used as a chantry for the family—that is a priest would be employed in saying Mass: this was the south transept chapel dedicated to St Stephen. The priest lived at Chantry House where now stands the Old Vicarage. The chantry was endowed with lands worth eleven pounds per year. "The incumbent thereof is one John Griffithe, Master of Arte and hath beside six pounds pension out of Hales monasteries, who teacheth there gramar to many young children." Though the endowment disappeared, Lade Anne Worsley, Sir John's daughter, re-endowed the school which was then held in Chantry House. Sir Richard Worsley gave the house to "The Free Grammar School". Later a Worsley was appointed headmaster, but sent a deputy to do the work! The present school house was built by Lord Yarborough in 1896 and is now a county junior school.

Several headmasters of the last century kept copious log-books which paint a vivid picture of the times, and show in particular how closely agriculture affected daily life. For example the main holiday was specifically for harvest and was seldom the same date two years running. In 1879 it ran from 30th August to 2nd October, but the following year it began on 3rd August. Whatever date school began again, attendance was always poor for several more weeks. A despairing entry for 1st October 1888 reads, "Gleaning not completed, half school absent, even after an extra week." Later, "October 24th, average attendance improving at last as children returning from field work."

Spring attendance was also vulnerable. "April 13th, several children asked leave to work at potato planting." One entry has an almost biblical ring: "March 16th. The day of humiliation. On account of cattle plague. The children attended church."

Many children came from outgoing farms—one boy walked three miles to school—so that bad weather could drastically affect numbers: in 1881 the school was closed for three weeks because of heavy snowfall. It was understandable then, that when several children asked for a half holiday on Shrove Tuesday, to go Shroving, it was not allowed. But for the races at nearby Appleford, a whole day's holiday was given.

In 1882, new schedules of payment for school came into force. These were, Labourer's children, twopence per week. Children of mechanics, gardeners etc., threepence. Children of yeomen, fourpence, though all under five were one penny. These were not always forthcoming. "George and Lottie repeatedly sent home for fees." A boy of twelve was admitted who had never been to school before.

On 13th April 1880, ". . . discontinued school fires, having no more coal belonging to school. Very cold. Children complain and would like fire." Accounts in the log-book show that coal was one shilling and fourpence (7p) a hundredweight. For cleaning and sweeping the school for twelve weeks the caretaker was paid nine shillings (45p).

Modernization begins to creep in. "October 4th 1878. Every sum given to Class II worked incorrectly, but every child had the same answer on his slate," but nine weeks later, "supplied every pupil with an exercise book, none of them having up to this time been accustomed to write on paper." (Many island schools went on using slates and slate pencils well into the present century.) Evening classes were sometimes held, though there were still attendance problems. In 1893 Mr Daniels commenced an evening class in botany.

Over the doorway stands the inscription "Godshill Parochial School founded by Lady Anne Worsley previous to 1615, rebuilt by the Right Honourable Lord Yarborough 1896".

Only a small percentage of visitors climb the steep hill to All Saints'. Those who do are rewarded, first of all by a lovely group of thatched cottages by the church entrance, one lovingly restored from condemned ruins, Old Bell Cottage which used to be the Bell Inn, the sexton's dwelling and another at one time a smallholding: it is thought this much-photographed group was originally built to house masons working on the church.

High on its knoll the church looks out over the cottages to a ring of green downland. Though there were earlier buildings on this site, perhaps even a pagan place of worship, All Saints' dates from the fourteenth century. The porch, however, brings one face to face with the present: on one side what appears to be a hunk of grey sponge, which turns out, frighteningly, to be a section of beam chewed by death-watch beetle: on the other, a hard-hitting quotation from T. S. Eliot's "Little Gidding":

You are not here to verify
Instruct yourself or inform curiosity
Or carry report. You are here to kneel.

This light and spacious church is nevertheless rich in historical detail. A rood beam marking the site of the old rood loft at once draws the eye. The north nave was probably the original parish church, while the south was added later by the monks of Appuldurcombe, the two then being separated by wooden screens fixed in the pillars of the arcade between. There are many memorials, some beautiful, some florid, to the owners of Appuldurcombe: a unique mural, the tattered colours of the Volunteers, or Home Guard of its time, raised against Napoleon, and an unusual modern memorial to a young soldier killed in the invasion of Normandy who had been a server at All Saints': this takes the form of a painted and gilded statue of St George.

Outside stand the remains of a fifteenth-century Rood cross, though the carved figures of the Crucifixion have long ago disappeared: now the top bears an eighteenth-century sundial. The oldest tombstone is said to be fourteenth century, though the oldest readable date is 1592.

Godshill church is one of the most beautiful on the island: one advantage to be gained from the felling of so many diseased elms round about, is a clearer view of it, dominating the land from this hilltop site chosen, according to the legend, by God himself.

From the village, walks lead enticingly in all directions. Sunken lanes banked with ferns and a field path lead over to the Whitwell Road and Bridgecourt, a fine seventeenth-century farmhouse. A footpath leads past it down to the valley of the Eastern Yar, here only a little stream in a green jungle of willow-herb, water mint and rushes overhung with ash and willow. A two-plank bridge leads across to the ruins of Bridgecourt Mill and cottage. One gable of the mill still stands with a tall sycamore growing from one corner: moss and hart's-tongue fern almost hide the remains of walls, though the axle and some spokes of the water wheel are still in place—Wordsworth would have loved such a romantic ruin. Walkers should wear boots. This path is part of the long-distance Worsley Trail which leads westward to the downs above Shorwell and Brighstone. The Stenbury Long Distance Trail can be picked up in Godshill Park and leads to Wroxall.

On the main road to Wroxall stands French Mill, attractively converted into a house, said to be named after the Norman monks who built it while at Appuldurcombe, or perhaps its first owner in 1285, de Francisco, a tenant of Sandford.

Wroxall village is a great contrast to Godshill: most of its main road houses are nineteenth century or later and no attempt at all is made to pretty them up. But if it lacks architectural charm, the village lies in an incomparable setting, deep in a fold between Stenbury and St Martin's Downs. Once again its derivation is open to question: in the Domesday survey it occurs as Warochesselle and one authority maintains this comes from the Anglo-Saxon *ceosel*, meaning gravel, but a more interesting one derives it from *wroc*, meaning a buzzard, a bird still sometimes to be seen over the island, circling on great blunt wings and doubtless far more common when the downs were really wild country.

Stenbury broods high above the village terminating on the north in a dramatic vertical fall, known as Gatcliff. Here there was once a quarry. When Henry VIII ordered alterations in Carisbrooke Castle, freestone from the Gatcliff quarries was used.

Otherwise for hundreds of years Wroxall was a small agricultural community with the Appuldurcombe estate providing extra work, and a bit of smuggling on the side. The pair of thatched cottages in the dip used to be a hiding place for barrels of spirit brought from Ventnor and Luccombe on their way to Newport.

In 1811 a "sudden and terrible fire broke out in a cottage belonging to one William Cole, which by the violence of the wind communicated to a dwelling house across a narrow lane and burnt down and destroyed the dwelling house, barn, stable, cowhouse together with the wagon . . . five loads of wheat, twelve quarters of barley". In all the total loss to William Jeffrey was reckoned to be seven hundred and forty pounds—a huge sum at that time, so a church brief or appeal was issued, to be read throughout the south of England. Over eight hundred pounds was raised, but the expenses of the appeal and the organizer's salary, reduced the amount to four hundred and fifteen pounds!

It was the coming of the railway which really changed the face of Wroxall. The Isle of Wight railway was incorporated in 1860 to build a coastal line from Ryde to Ventnor, linking the ferry terminal with the main holiday resorts. The St John's Ryde to Shanklin stretch was opened in 1864, with plans for its extension through Luccombe and the Undercliff to Bonchurch and Ventnor. At this time Ventnor was rapidly becoming an important health resort because of its mild climate: the enormous Royal National Hospital was to be built in 1868.

But Lord Yarborough, of Appuldurcombe, objected as well he might to a railway being ploughed through the coastal lands under the steep slopes of St Boniface Down: the line could not go over, so it had to go *through*. It was built round the curve of the down to Wroxall, then tunnelled through the hills. A tunnel thirteen hundred yards long needed an army of workmen, some brought over from the mainland; many of the houses in the main street were built for them.

At the opening, engines were decked with flowers and flags and one train ran an hour late because of all the merry-making. A Shanklin lady was moved to write:

Hark! Hark! I hear a whistle shrill
And lo the puffing steam
All over hedge and through the hill
What—am I in a dream!

Wroxall was originally a mere halt, but was enlarged into a station in 1925.

While the tunnel was being excavated, one workman's pick struck a pottery vessel which cracked open and spilled out "a great number" of Roman coins from about the fourth century A.D., known afterwards as the Wroxall Hoard. A writer in the *Gentleman's Magazine* of that time says, "I use the word residue as best explaining what I saw, for although the number of coins turned up from the soil was very large, they have been so dispersed among the labourers and cottagers of the neighbourhood that only a few hundred remain. When the mass of coins was first thrown out, the finder (who appears to have an extra amount of dullness) shovelled them among the earth which was being moved to another part of the works . . . those found being mostly brass or copper."

But anyone familiar with the island temperament and quick-witted tricks of hard-pressed smugglers, will at once recognize the finder as having an extra presence of mind!

To cope with the new population, the first church in Wroxall was erected. Hill's *Directory* for 1871 describes it as a temporary wooden structure dedicated to St Michael. However, after the building of the tunnel an abundance of quarried stone was at hand, and this was used to build the Church of St John which stands in the High Street, a handsome building with a conical tower displaying a large blue clock. The tunnel-stone has not worn well and needs constant repair: fortunately bombs aimed at the Radar Station on the summit of St Boniface only shook St John's and it retains six stained-glass windows. Wroxall became an independent parish only as late as 1907.

After the closure of the Ventnor to Shanklin line in 1965, the station building lay disused for a period, but was eventually dismantled. On its site arose a custom-built Community Centre, opened by Lord Louis Mountbatten, Governor of the Island, in 1978. Besides incorporating a doctor's surgery, this really has become a centre of village life, used for lectures and discos, bazaars and club meetings, badminton and a variety of handicrafts such as pewter and lace making which flourish particularly in the Wroxall area, while a Travel Club organizes trips abroad.

Appuldurcombe is well signposted though bowered in trees under Stenbury Down and not visible from the village street: Worsley Road (with a view of a large camping site) and Yarborough Terrace are further reminders. A stranger might well think there is a second historic monument when he sees Castle Garage and Castle Road, but the names refer to a folly, built on the downs to improve the Worsleys' view, of which only a few stones now remain. It is still a pleasant walk though.

Castle Road turns up towards St Martin's Down and almost at once mounts a bridge over the old railway line. Here stands a large stone complex of buildings; on the lower one—once facing the trains—can still be read a faded sign, "The Isle of Wight Bacon Factory, Flux and Sons", while round the back of the four-storey mill a notice reads "For miller please ring", though both have been closed more than ten years. Local children used to be told a pig was put in at one end of the factory and sausages emerged at the other, while older residents still say: "They don't make sausages like them any more." Part of the old buildings are used by the small industrial estate which is growing up here—an electronics factory sits right across the old railway line.

Another startling change of use can be seen in the main street. The Bible Christian Movement was very strong in central Wight, having an early meeting place in a cottage at Rookley. In Wroxall they eventually built a large chapel. With its tall windows bricked up against traffic noise, this has become a recording studio.

The Methodists still flourish though and enjoy very friendly relations with the Church of England close by. The big new housing estates which cover even the lower slope of down must bring an influx of population equal to that of the nineteenth-century tunnel builders. In a quiet road near Appuldurcombe entrance there is a new garden of great interest, sometimes open to the public.

A long lawn looks across to the heights of Stenbury Down, but the eye is drawn to the nearer view of borders and a series of formal circular beds bright with flowers at all times of year, in summer with asters and begonias, fuchsias and roses for example, while on the terrace below is the vegetable garden: two ponds hold goldfish and lilies—pretty, one might think, but hardly remarkable on an island renowned for its gardens. But look again. Aren't the dahlias brighter than the usual ones, the peas more succulent looking?

The garden at Park View was created in 1976 and has been cultivated ever since on the Bio-Dynamic principles laid down by Rudolph Steiner, organic gardening taken one step further. A giant compost heap is the heart of the matter: though a rotting agent is used it will itself be organically based, as will the insecticides and fertilizers. The idea is to build up the health of the plants naturally so that they become resistant to pests and diseases, while the phases of the moon and the planets also play a part.

Wroxall is the centre of a whole network of lovely downland walks leading to Ventnor, Shanklin and Godshill. One of the best starts with Manor Road because it shows what Old Wroxall was like. On the right corner stands the Star Inn, just rebuilt after a disastrous fire, on the other a fine stone drinking trough and fountain, inscribed "Metropolitan Drinking Fountain and Cattle Trough Association"—alas containing dead grass. The lane soon leaves new building behind. Below runs a stream and the old railway line now overgrown with mayweed and thorn bushes, with here and there a stone cottage, and two farms with huge old barns and outbuildings. Beyond Wroxall Cross the lane branches into footpaths that lead high over the downs south and east. Paths westward from the village lead over to Whitwell.

Tradition says this village is named from the White Well to which pilgrimages were made in medieval times. A spring rose on the land of Ash Farm which would produce a hundred barrels of pure fine water in an hour; while the name Ash is said to be derived from a Celtic word for source. A well is still to be seen, though not a spring: while it stands under a new stone wall and suffers the indignity of a wire grid, one can peer down through the moss and ferns at its rim to a pool of clear water below.

The well lies just off the south end of the High Street, which slopes down from the church in a valley between the downs. Though large new housing estates lie behind the street, the village is less urbanized than Wroxall, lines a much quieter road and is largely unknown to the tourist trade, while the architecture is splendidly varied with many old houses. The thatched and whitewashed White Horse pub, parts of which are fifteenth century, claims to be the oldest pub on the island; there is stone and thatch of 1722, brick cottages of 1867, the old forge still in use by a firm of welding engineers, a V.R. post box, as well as a filling station and bungalows and some new houses faced with stone.

What now looks like a terrace of cottages was once the Church House: old photographs show it with stone mullions and diamond panes now disappeared. In the sixteenth century it was a kind of club house for the village, let out by the churchwardens. A proviso in the lease said, "Provided always that if the quarter shall need at any time to make a church-ale, for the maintenance of the chapel that it shall be lawful for them to have the use of the said house, with all the rooms both above and beneath during their ale"—an ale being the sale of one brewing and a general merry-making. A gallon of beer was provided for the bishop when he visited.

Even if the White Well provided ample water, for beer making and other needs, it was a long climb from the north end of the village. In 1887 Whitwell was provided with water standards by a Mr Spindler of St Lawrence which was then in this parish. These handsome iron pillars, each with bucket stand at foot and a drinking cup on a chain, issued forth water from the mouth of a benevolent-looking lion: several of them remain, painted red, along the High Street.

Whitwell's sheltered valley with a stream running through it is thought to have been the site of a Saxon village with an open field system. Later the land was cultivated on the strip system, where a householder would hold several half-acre plots in different large fields, with the right to graze on common land. The village originally belonged to the Norman de Estur family as part of their estate at Gatcombe, some five miles distant. The patron saint of this family was St Rhadegunde, a German princess, who, after being kidnapped into France, escaped from court life to found a nunnery and devote her life to the care of beggars and lepers.

Whitwell church must own the strangest history of any on the island, since it was once *two* separate buildings. The northern and oldest part was originally a memorial chapel built for their tenants by the de Estur family of Gatcombe and naturally dedicated to St Rhadegunde, in the twelfth century. (The old path used by worshippers from the south is still called by her name though locally reduced to Radgons, just as the village name becomes Wittle, or something ruder.) In the next century the Lords of Stenbury built a self-contained chapel on to the south side, retaining the solid wall between, for their tenants in St Lawrence: this was dedicated to the Blessed Virgin Mary.

Not till the sixteenth century was the dividing wall taken down and the church enlarged—there is a mason's mark on the south wall: RMN, 1589. When the tower was added, extra supporting arches were added at the west end. Today Whitwell is a beautiful little church, with its short castellated tower and ancient grey stones surrounded by a graveyard and old walls sprouting marguerites and fern. Inside, a knowledge of its curious history adds interest to the strange arch within an arch, and the different dedications of the naves. A wealth of richly toned stained-glass windows warm the interior. Look out for a great bell standing at the west end, a pair of carved hands, toddler size but bearing stigmata, found in the roof during a Victorian restoration and a water-colour of a curious wall painting found at the same time which unfortunately crumbled away on exposure. A group of Eastern figures bearing scimitars contemplate a slit and headless corpse, with temples in the background and the head of a dragon: the martyrdom of St Erasmus has been suggested.

The present bells and clock were the gift of William Spindler whose tall marble monument in the churchyard used to have railings round it and certainly deserves more than the six-foot nettles which obscure it from sight at the moment.

A stretch of marshy ground, known as Rush Butt, used to provide rushes both to cover the floor of the church, before pews were introduced, and to light it: for this the soft green was stripped off, then the spine of the leaf dipped in wax and left to cool.

Next door to the churchyard stands a curious monastic-looking house with tall three-storey gables, "lancet" windows, even stained glass, but it turns out to be merely the old vicarage, built in 1868, now a Youth Hostel with thirty-one beds. Nettlecombe Lane in the middle of the High Street is a good starting point for walks.

The road leads to the old station, now a private dwelling: by the entrance stands a large house at one time The Yarborough Arms, but then the way narrows to a steep lane leading up to the hamlet of Nettlecombe, a cluster of old cottages and farm buildings: (Mr Spindler's water lions reached right up here). From the slope of Stenbury there are wide views westward to the long green lines of St Catherine's Down with the tall Hoy Monument at its northern end—but the view below is of all the new building behind Whitwell High Street: only now does it make a real visual impact, seeming to swamp the old village.

Whitwell is by no means the only island village with such estates so what impact does all this building have? Here it is worth considering what Whitwell was like a hundred years ago. While it had good communications, that is a carrier's van to Newport four times a week and twice to Ventnor as well as the railway and horse traffic, the village was largely self-supporting, a small stream worked two mills north of the High Street, there were dairymen, grocers, butchers, a baker, a dressmaker, two shoemakers, a builder, carpenter, two blacksmiths and various farms supplying eggs, poultry and dairy food.

Gradually this has changed—children find it hard to believe that shoes were *made* in their village: more and more young people went to work in towns in service industries, yet most families had deep roots. When a brand-new estate is plonked down beside a village, almost no one in it is going to work locally. This can create two communities rather than one larger one: new householders commute to work, shop in towns; the school which might bring old and new residents together has long been derelict but is now being repaired and turned into a community centre which will perhaps have that effect.

On the other hand, many villages in the early twentieth century had become literally inbred communities, needing new blood and new ideas. It is often people who have retired to the island from the mainland who inject new talent into dramatic societies, musical life and parish activities.

The farms remain—here up at Nettlecombe the hens still range free. There is a choice of downland walks both leading to interesting old farms. Northwards, lanes and fields lead over to Godshill, passing Stenbury Manor, a fine old house on an ancient site. Here lived the Norman family de Aula, and later the De Heynos who probably built the moated house which once stood east of the present site. Eventually it was bought by the Worsleys of Appuldurcombe who pulled down the old house and built a new one in the eighteenth century. When the moat was being filled in, Sir Richard Worsley wrote in his history, "There were found ten earthen pots or urns filled up with coals and bits of bones: from the different composition, shape and size of urns, the spot might probably have been a family cemetery."

Southward from Nettlecombe a path leads over to Dean Farm on the Ventnor road: a farm of this name paid taxes in 1327: the present one, a beautiful stone dwelling and complex of barns, dates from the eighteenth century. Opposite, by the old railway crossing, St Rhadegund's Path leads south to the Undercliff or west to Niton.

Great rivalry used to exist between Whitwell and Niton, a relic of smuggling days. If a Niton youth courted a Whitwell girl, his mates would throw him in the duck pond, after which he was free to continue his courting. If a lone Niton chap came into Whitwell to catch a train, he was liable to be pelted with clods on the way, to shouts of "A Nit'ner, a Nit'ner". The last prisoner in Whitwell stocks, which used to stand outside the church, was, naturally, a Nit'ner.

6

Undercliff and Landslip

Beneath the Upper Greensand and chalk of the massive southern hills lurks Gault clay, known locally and with good reason as Blue Slipper. Over thousands of years, as wet clay oozed out from beneath, leaving the heavier rocks unsupported, this has caused gigantic landslips: the Undercliff is a six-mile terrace formed in this way, sheltered from the north-west by a high inland cliff where the land broke off sheer, and terracing down to low sea cliffs, a country bowered in trees with a climate mild enough to grow fuchsias, camellias, even bananas!

Niton is the only village with a foot in either camp, as it were. Upper Niton lies in a bare hollow of the downs, while Barrack Shute plunges down to Lower Niton at the western end of the Undercliff road. Upper Niton today clusters round a crossroads where routes inland cross those along the coast: a variety of shops, even a bank, cannot prevent the village retaining its pleasant rural atmosphere, new buildings at least in the centre being far outnumbered by old stone, thatch or Victorian cottages, while a simple one-way traffic system syphons off much heavy traffic on the coastal route at the southern end of the High Street.

One might easily guess that Niton had grown up round this crossroads—and be wrong. That busy road over the western cliff to Chale is comparatively new, built between the wars after a landslide destroyed the lower road,* while the village itself goes back to Domesday and beyond. Then it was called Neeton, and a little later Newton: the church was one of the six given to the abbey of Lyra in Normandy by William Fitz-Osborn.

To visualize medieval Niton, one must rethink the whole village shape. There was never a manor house, the most important dwelling being Manor Farm next door to the church, in front of which spread the village green dominated by a tall cross, while just above, a large pond fed a stream which trickled through the village eastwards. Older residents can remember skating on the pond, picking watercress from the beds beside it, or falling in the sheep dip. It seems a pity the stream had to disappear when the pumping station was built. It is in fact the infant Eastern Yar which rose nearby and now proceeds in a series of culverts, to be glimpsed here and there, such as the corner of Laceys Lane. This gives rise to houses named Springhead and Brookside standing in apparently waterless lanes. The pond is a marshy jungle overgrown with ivy and bindweed, ash and sycamore, under which the walls of the sheep-dip can just be traced.

The oldest part of the church of St John the Baptist is the eleventh-century nave: traces of a Norman north aisle disappeared when a new one was built in an extensive Victorian restoration, incorporating four lancet windows of bright stained glass—the east window is small and renders the chancel rather dark. A Norman font with a cable-pattern rim is still in use. Over the churchyard wall one may glimpse the Manor Farm house, part of it fifteenth century. Many old gravestones have been removed and reused as flagstones for paths, but a pink marble memorial remains: this is in memory of Edward Edwards, "man of letters", one of the founders of the public library system. The medieval stone pedestal, five courses high, now surmounted by a nineteenth-century cross, provides a fine view point over the village, for the church stands on a little knoll: one can look out right over thatch and slate roofs to the downlands beyond, and cows grazing above the village.

For hundreds of years Niton was a farming and fishing village. In summer a watch was kept for shoals of mackerel swimming up the English Channel, then a community catch went into operation. One end of a long net was held on shore, while the other was rowed out to make a wall, at right angles to the shore, ahead of the shoal. When the mackerel swam up to the net, the seaward end was rowed back to shore westward so the fish were caught in a great semicircular bag which was then dragged ashore—fish caught in this way were held to have better flavour than those which died in the sea. Crabs were always plentiful too. A fish market was held on the green every Wednesday and Friday, and a Midsummer Fair ending with a dance at the White Lion. "That honest recreation was very common, and not dishonourable but as a means to make many matches and to draw much company together, ye gayne whereof went to ye maintenance of ye church," wrote Sir John Oglander.

This is a description of the village in about 1800: every cottage had enough land to grow vegetables and keep a pig, some had orchards as well for cider making. Twelve farmers owned all the land, the other men worked for them, communally at harvest time: no women went out to work, they did not even spin or knit, but were said to be outstanding mothers. Cut off from any towns—there was no carriage road to Newport—the villagers were reckoned a "pretty rough lot", or as Dr Whitehead delicately phrases it, "Separated from the great world . . . under such circumstances the manners, the appearance, the mode of life of these secreted villagers could not fail of being strongly tinctured with the cast of originality."

A hundred years later that picture is much changed. Ventnor had become a health resort: the Undercliff's romantic beauty had been discovered: the wealthy built "cottages" large ornate houses such as Mirables, Puckaster and Mount Cleves, and laid out large grounds looking to the sea. When Niton girls left school they would go and work as maids, for a large house would employ eight or nine. Boys who didn't want to go on the land could work as gardeners, house staff or as builders' labourers. There was also a growing need for transport which created employment. Four horse coaches would meet trains at Whitwell to distribute visitors and a regular wagonette service ran from Chale, through Niton to Ventnor. Two brickyards at Bierley, north of the village, turned out bricks for the new building craze, sending four hundred bricks out in each cartload: these were supplemented by others brought by train to Whitwell and sometimes delivered by traction engines. At other times these were used by farmers to drive threshing machines, each farmer supplying his own coal.

Even children could make a few pennies opening gates for the rich folk: at Easter they picked primroses and threw them to the visitors who responded with coppers. Older boys would run to the post office after school to see if any telegrams needed delivery; the going rate was twopence for delivering in the Undercliff, three pence for Blackgang, a three-mile walk—but then you could buy a pound of sprats for twopence, and ten herrings for a shilling.

With the 1914 war and the men away fighting, fishing came almost to a halt, and never did regain its old importance, though the war brought another kind of harvest. Niton men had always been great beachcombers: now from torpedoed ships there rolled in a wildly varied flotsam, butter and lard, tins of cigarettes, grapes and oranges, sacks of flour and highly prized tins of beef.

This is a typical day in the life of a Niton boy who left school, as was customary, at thirteen and went to work at Mirables, ten hours a day but only eight on Sundays, for seven shillings a week. It was 1916.

As he lived in Upper Niton, he had to be up at five. Having walked the miles down to Mirables he had to feed and groom the horse, fill the cart with milk churns and drive it along to Underwath, a convalescent home for soldiers, in St Lawrence—if it had snowed in the night he would have to take a shovel to clear the road. The milk had to be in time for the patients' seven-thirty breakfast. After driving back and washing out the churns, he could buy an egg for a penny and boil it for breakfast in a shed. During the rest of the morning he would collect the kitchen swill to feed the pigs, work in the fields or break in horses. At dinner time he'd slip down to the shore to see what had come in on the last tide. In the afternoon there was another milk delivery and the dairy washing. Finally when he'd fed the horse and cleaned out its stable there was the long steep walk home up Barrack Shute.

Until then the most famous wreck had been the *Russie*, since her cargo was largely wine and spirits. When this began to come ashore the locals broached the tubs then and there but much of the contents was too strong even for Niton stomachs and many fell asleep or stupefied on the beach! But in 1917, a winter of deep deprivation with the staple food black bread, *La Peruz* ran aground at Puckaster Cove a few hundred feet from shore.

When her lights were glimpsed through the December twilight the word went round the village "Wreck in Puckaster!" but four tugs were sent round to tow her off. They tried on each high tide for two days but in vain. Finally she began to jettison cargo, huge rolls of paper, tubs of lubricating oil and best of all, boxes of pork joints. Next day, carts, wagons, wheelbarrows, even prams, began to converge on Niton from far and near. In Niton, pork was hidden in cellars, attics, waterbutts, but the excise carried out rigorous searches and many were fined.

The wisest local family simply grabbed as many boxes as they could, hauled them above high-water line and painted "Salvaged by Morris" on each one. Later the boxes were hauled up to Mirables on sledges and declared to the Customs Officer. The family received a salvage reward of fifty pounds—worth several hundred in these days. Soon after a flu epidemic ravaged the island, but the Nitoners seemed immune, presumably too well set up on pork fat to catch germs.

There used to be five pubs in the village, now only the White Lion remains, in the centre, its low-beamed ceilings and horse brasses evoking the proper country atmosphere but there is also a jazz night every week, and an up-to-date restaurant.

One of the prettiest old thatched cottages is Nutkins, bought in 1919 by Aubrey de Selincourt and his home for many years where he wrote distinguished translations of the classics and some delightful children's stories set on the Isle of Wight.

The village used to be known as Crab Niton, to distinguish it from Knighton, usually pronounced Kaynighton, near Newchurch; naturally the Whitters said Crab was put on because "they'm a crabby ol' lot, over Nitton", while locals maintain it refers to the rich catches along the beaches of Lower Niton, the village below the inner cliff, a "Majestic perpendicular which has kept its station and forms the northern boundary of this truly romantic spot, presents the appearance of the walls of an old castle many hundred feet in height curiously fretted into rock work and picturesquely interspersed with lichens, ivy and other creeping plants".

A lane to the west, hung with trees, leads past the Sandrock Hotel, built in 1790 with a beautiful lawn terrace looking to the Channel. Princess Victoria once stayed here to drink the spring waters, after which Royal was of course added to its name. Later, Signor Marconi stayed here while carrying out his pioneer wireless experiments. The lane leads on into more open cliff country and the lighthouse on St Catherine's Point, the island's southernmost extremity, and beloved of bird-watchers. Sidney Dobell, an undervalued poet of the nineteenth century, often spent winters in the milder Undercliff climate and wrote of the Point, "We have had strange apparitions of birds lately—migrations I suppose . . . there passed every morning for an hour innumerable armies, all flying from west to east. Most of them dark, but officered by large white gulls with black tips to their wings."

Turning east, past a terrace of houses built out of stone cleared from their site, one comes to the Buddle Inn, well known for good food, a quaint old building but only a pub since the nineteenth century. Buddle is an island word meaning stream, and one flows through the garden, but in 1776 it was called Bundle Place, bundle meaning a parcel of land. Another theory maintains that the name is derived from a trough used in tin mining, since it was widely held at one time (through the similarity of the name Ictis to Vectis) that tin from Cornwall mined in Roman times was brought to Hampshire, across a causeway to Gurnard and across the island to be shipped from Puckaster Cove, that name derived from Port Castor. (Today the Roman name for the island survives in the Vectis Bus Company.) At one time Niton possessed The Cat and Rabbit, the Blue Lion and the more recently closed Star.

Lanes and paths lead down to the shore. Below small cliffs all this coast is divided up into small rocky coves, some hardly accessible from land, though at the nearest, Castle Cove, there is a cottage, boathouse and a narrow channel out through the reef. Puckaster lies round the point eastwards.

During the Commonwealth period, the Rector of Niton, an ardent loyalist, was deprived of his parish but was allowed to return at the Restoration, so what must have been his delight when the monarch was brought to his door, literally "by an ill wind". The church register bears on its fly leaf, "July 1st, 1675, Charles the Second, King of Great Britain, France and Ireland etc., came safely ashore at Puckaster, after he had endured a great and dangerous storm at sea. That he may reign long and happily Thomas Collinson prays and ardently desires." According to an island ballad, the King set foot on shore:

And then turning to old Collinson,
He said how he full well knew
That his deeds of faithful loyalty
Had been neither small nor few—

and asked if he might spend the night at the Rectory.

Cove after cove, secret channels through the rocks, above the cliffs, country jumbled into hillocks and hollows, copses and lanes—this account of Niton has so far left out one deeply important subject—smuggling, because it belongs to the whole coastal stretch rather than one village. Smuggling was no occasional romantic escapade, but a chief means of livelihood, indeed survival, along the south-east and south-west coasts. This despairing letter from a Customs Officer in 1886 paints a vivid picture of the general condition on the island.

"We have sixty eight men, eighteen to work by day and fifty at night, which is totally inadequate to prevent them running goods almost whenever and wherever they please—even if it were possible for our men to keep alert for sixteen hours, which is the time they are often on the beach." There was such a glut of spirits on the island that it was cheaper to buy here than anywhere else in Britain and there was a thriving "export" trade to the mainland with fifty boats constantly plying across the Solent. It was reckoned that three out of four Niton families were involved in smuggling: from court papers it is known that some of the smugglers were in fact excise men and even a boy of eleven was convicted of carrying a quart of contraband brandy.

The boats were usually rowed across to the French coast with a crew of six or eight at night: each boat would bring back up to fifty four-gallon tubs of spirit which were secreted away in caves, buried or brought up an underground passage from the shore into thick woodland, till they could be safely removed and the spirit treated—that is diluted with an equal quantity of water and coloured with burnt sugar. Great community spirit—if that is the word—existed, since posters were often put up offering five hundred pounds' reward for information laid, an enormous sum in the eighteenth century.

Even so, the nosy had to be kept away. Smugglers' ruses have led to all kinds of ghost stories about the Undercliff road—phantom horses, skeletons with beating hearts, even a ghost coach. The horse was achieved with whitewash and special hoof pads which were used anyway to muffle sound: similarly a skeleton could be painted with whitewash on old dark clothes—the heart was a small drum. Puckaster Cove was a haunt of fairies, children were told. If you saw a light down there, it was "Puck's little midnight star". Easy to laugh now, but even today with tarmac underfoot and houses never far away, the Undercliff road can still be a strange place at night, trees arching overhead, the great cliff inland rearing black against the stars, huge masses of fallen jumbled rock looming up on the broken ground falling away to the sea.

Today it is difficult to know where Lower Niton merges into St Lawrence, but the nucleus of the latter village was never on the coast road: it must be sought up the steep shute now called Seven Sisters Road, the original main route from St Lawrence to the world above. Here stands the old church of St Lawrence. After the conquest, the estate was given to the Norman de Aula family who built themselves a chapel round which grew a very small settlement. Early references are sparse. In Henry III's reign one reads of "Robert de Whytewell having slain Henry Etene in the vell of St Lawrence and being accordingly outlawed". Later it belonged to the Worsleys of Appuldurcombe, thence to the Yarboroughs and Pelhams. When the Rector listed the families living in the parish in 1756, there were eleven houses, counting the Poor House, but by the 1811 census there were fourteen houses, and eighteen families, about eighty residents.

A tragic entry in the church register for 1799 reads, "A young man named Morey and a young woman Jane Saunders, were killed by part of the cliff falling upon them at the time of a shipwreck—The Three Sisters, a West Indian ship—and buried with the bodies of nine mariners and one passenger drowned."

By this time smuggling was rife, in spite of the Napoleonic Wars. Amongst the group of cottages round the church stood one called The Duck, where cheap spirits could be bought day or night. (Five coastguards were sent to St Lawrence in 1818 and a proper coastguard station built on the cliffs in 1855.)

At Vestry Cottage the rector robed up for service because the church was so small: it was also used as a school before a larger house was found and eventually the purpose-built school erected in 1898, now the village hall.

Outside the community round the church were scattered single large houses in wide grounds. The earliest of these must be ruins in the grounds of Wolverton Manor, for long referred to as a chapel because of its window shapes, but modern research has shown them to be the remains of a thirteenth-century dwelling house, possibly built by the de Aulas.

Sir Richard Worsley of Appuldurcombe built what he modestly named The Cottage, an eighteenth-century mansion now let into several flats. In the drive he erected St Lawrence Well, having captured the waters of the original spring which rose to the north, here described in a Victorian guide. "I could have gazed for a long time on its arched entrance, its groined roof, its ivy clustered walls and rustic seat. The water falls from a dolphin's head ino a wide grooved shell at the back of the cool, cell like retreat amid hanging willows." The small chapel-like building is still there and may be readily visited since a public footpath runs past, but iron gates bar entry and all wears a cobwebbed air of neglect.

As Ventnor grew in importance as a health resort, the beauties of the Undercliff began to be appreciated and a new level road terracing along beneath the inner cliff but through the hanging woods, soon became a popular carriage route to Blackgang, and a desirable place to build a country residence—Mirables is one such with its conical roofed turrets. In a way these houses, with their vast grounds parts of which were left in their wild state of old woods and jumbled mossy boulders, have done a great deal to conserve the character of St Lawrence and Niton: even so there has been so much modern building local people fear that any more would really tame the Undercliff.

Such a romantic spot was bound to draw writers to its green shades. Swinburne used to stay with his cousin at The Orchard. Mrs Pearl Craigie, a well-known Victorian novelist under the name John Oliver Hobbs, rented a house called St Lawrence Lodge, from Mr Spindler at Old Park, who designed an Italian garden for her use there. After her death the house was renamed

Craigie Lodge and a memorial tablet set in the gatepost. East of Orchard's Bay, Turgenev the Russian novelist began to write *Fathers and Sons*. Jean Ingelow, most famous for her poem "High Tide on the Coast of Lincolnshire", wrote another long balled called "The Letter L" set in a cove below:

The Pelham woods
Were full of doves that cooed at ease;
The orchis filled her purple
For dainty bees.

Alice Meynell used to stay near Steephill Castle, now sadly demolished, but Lisle Combe remains, the beloved home of Alfred Noyes,* of which he wrote, "At the first glimpse, there was a sense of homecoming—forty acres of the Hesperides and unspoilable. It lies between two wooded promontories, faces due south, undulating softly to a wide meadow yellow with cowslips in spring." (The garden is occasionally opened in summer.)

Old Park which lies lower down, below the woods, above cliff meadows is not a literary shrine, but has a long history. Sir John Oglander wrote in the seventeenth century, "The Undercliff swarmed with game—partridge, pheasants, curlews, plovers, gulls, and other wild fowl." It was in fact one of the three medieval parks or hunting grounds on the island, the others being at Wootton and Carisbrooke. Old Park itself belonged to the ubiquitous Worsleys and later to William Spindler. He came originally to Ventnor to recover from a breakdown in health, and fell in love with this part of the island. "Ventnor saved my life," he would often say and in gratitude he determined to "improve" it. In a small book written in 1873 he complained of the number of stone walls, the lack of trees and the general air of *manana*, or let's do it tomorrow.

Being a man of action, he bought Old Park and drew up plans for a new port and village to extend from it to Ventnor. While it was perhaps fortunate for the Undercliff that he died before much of this plan could be put into action, it is sad that his name is remembered locally only for chunks of ruined sea wall known as Spindlers Folly, for William Spindler was a generous benefactor, bringing water, as noted in Chapter Five, to everyone in Whitwell, giving a peal of six bells to Whitwell church and planting thousands of trees.

Today Old Park is a residential hotel with two attractions enjoyed by many day visitors. In the studio you can stand in the red glare and roar of the furnace to watch delicate glassware being blown, whilst behind some of those high walls abominated by Mr Spindler, you can stroll through the aviaries of the bird park on intimate terms with toucans, macaws and weavers or idle by the lake to watch cranes, spoonbills and storks.

Seven Sisters Road continues up the steep shute which climbs the inner cliff and used to be the road to Newport. A handful of beautiful stone cottages remain bowered in trees and just past the village pump in its grotto lies the old church, an enchanting little building seeming sunken into the ground, its walls a mere six feet high. From its graveyard the view extends over the tree tops below to the cliff meadows and the sea. The church was probably built as a chapel by the de Aulas: the list of Rectors begins simply "1201. Roger."

Inside, the low ceiling, dark beams and plain walls speak of its great age: until the chancel was lengthened by Lord Yarborough in 1842, St Lawrence claimed to be the smallest church in England—it is still very small. John Green the parish clerk, writing before the addition, claimed it to be the smallest in the British Dominions. His verses end on an ominous note:

. . . though the building is so low and small
You may be near to Heaven as at St. Paul.
Its length is sixty feet, breadth forty two
And there the dead do meet to wait for you.

A tall man would need to stoop entering the south door: the lintel of the north now blocked up is even lower. An absent-minded rector, living at Chale, was peacefully mending his crab pots when a passer-by remarked it was a fine Sunday. Realizing he should be in church, the priest rode over to St Lawrence and rushing in to church by the north door, struck his head on the stone and was killed. (A much newer and larger church stands beside the Undercliff road.)

Just above the old church stands the old station house. The railway was opened in 1897, after the blasting of the tunnel through the downs from Whitwell. "The melodies of nature in the churchyard are now broken in upon by the none too tuneful locomotive," said a guide of the time: the railway was closed in

1952, and part of the line is now being used for new housing. Indeed new houses cluster all around the old, but at least the lush growth of trees and shrubs soon helps to clothe and soften raw new edges.

St Francis, for example, a little further west, is bowered in hydrangeas, but so are many other houses. St Francis is special, though, known all over the island as a bird hospital. Spring is the busiest time when lost and abandoned nestlings are brought in; cat-damaged garden birds arrive all the year round, together with exhausted carrier pigeons, hawks and owls with hurt wings from flying into cables, and gulls suffering from botulism. Sebastian, a black swan attacked by a rat as a fledgling, is a resident because he can never fly, but the real aim is to return birds to the wild, never to tame them.

A sick bird is first of all put in a warm dark box and left alone to recover from shock, then fed: fledglings thrive on a mixture of fine biscuit meal, raw meat, cheese and honey. Blackbirds and owls are some of the easiest to treat whereas starlings are bundles of nerves and often die of shock. After treatment they live in aviaries in the garden till well enough to fly off. The rarest patient in 1981 was a wryneck, found at Wroxall with a bruised wing.

Oiled sea birds present an entirely different problem: the winter of 1980-1 was the worst so far with three hundred oiled guillemots and razorbills being washed up along the Undercliff coast. Until recently the success rate for returning to the sea was low, but now a new technique has been pioneered by Leeds University in which each bird is sprayed with hand-hot detergent, then rinsed in clear water of the same heat until the natural oils can actually be seen returning to the feathers and waterproofing them. By this method birds can often be returned to the sea after a week whereas by the old method it could be months before they achieved buoyancy. It must be emphasized that no amateur should try the new technique without training. There are contingency plans that in a real emergency, island birds would be taken to a centre in the West Country for expert treatment.

Not only birds come to St Francis; deserted leverets are brought up on bottles of baby food, and fox cubs mothered by the cat; no hurt thing fur or feathered is ever turned away, but it is always a small celebration when a hawk returns to air from the high cliff, or a razorbill to the sea.

From the Undercliff road many lanes and paths lead out across the humpy green sea cliffs, though fewer lead down to the shore for the cliffs are steep, rising up here and there in miniature tors which form beautiful natural rock gardens in summer covered with kidney vetch, bird's-foot trefoil, mats of purple thyme, while samphire and the rare hoary stock grow on the cliff face.

The coves below are a jumble of dark rocks, pale pebbles and stretches of sand, a rewarding ground for the fossil hunter, ammonites being common in rock debris under the cliffs. Black-headed gulls squabble out on the reefs, the commonest sea birds along this coast, with herring gulls and cormorants as frequent passers-by. From the exhilarating cliff path the view changes all the time as another small headland is reached: westward, St Catherine's Lighthouse shines white on the island's most southerly point.

Eastward the cliff path leads on to Ventnor, but a side branch leads down into the Botanic Gardens,* a sheltered parkland once the grounds of the Royal National Hospital for Diseases of the Chest, now the home of many exotic plants including palms and bananas. The hospital itself was demolished to ground level, but the boiler houses, fuel store and refrigeration room remained as they are deep underground. These dark vaulted cellars have been turned into a most atmospheric Museum of Smuggling.

Here can be seen the reality that underlay the legends—pads for horses' hooves, a spade handle with a horseshoe on the end for making misleading tracks, a spout-lantern whose light could be seen out at sea but not on land, and all the different means of slinging barrels round boats so that they could be jettisoned in a hurry, together with grapnels for recovering them. But the museum is concerned with the whole history of smuggling in England, beginning rather surprisingly, with the smuggling of wool *out* of England in the thirteenth century: while spirit is the commodity which always springs to mind, goods smuggled in included tea, tobacco, bales of silk—one memorable item is a finely stitched soft leather glove, brought ashore in a walnut shell. Show-cases devoted to the twentieth century show wildly ingenious ways of smuggling in drugs, watches, diamonds, money—and people. The museum does not neglect to show smuggling as an often brutal way of life leading to gang fights, even the murder of customs officers, and punished by equal brutality. For a complete change of atmosphere one should go and take tea in the rose garden beside the fountain and water lilies.

The romantic beauty of the Undercliff has always inspired artists: today St Lawrence has a flourishing Art Society which holds frequent exhibitions in Ventnor.

On the other side of that town lies Bonchurch—one might take it for a leafy suburb since the two are now entwined, but Ventnor is comparatively new, whereas the history of Bonchurch claims its own beacon to light the Dark Ages.

All through the Undercliff, landslides have from time to time revealed long-buried rubbish heaps, fascinating evidence of the life of early man: one such heap at Bonchurch contained limpet and winkle shells, the bones of oxen and horses, the tusk of a wild boar and horns from a red deer. On the downs above a group of burial mounds was excavated in 1855 and found to contain urns of a very early period, unbaked, which fell to pieces on exposure to the air. Roman burial urns have been found in Niton, Ventnor and Bonchurch and a Roman camp is said to have existed on the cliff edge before this fell away.

Though it is known that the Saxons invaded the island in the sixth century, island history at this time is obscure, but this fishing hamlet claims its story and its very name date from about 700. In A.D. 680, a baby was born in Crediton, Devon, and christened Winfrith: he determined to become a man of God and when he grew up, entered a Hampshire monastery where he was given the name Boniface or "doer of good". Later he was sent to Germany, became Bishop of Mainz, but at some time, tradition avers, he came to the Undercliff, preached to the people and founded the church called after him, Bone-cerce, Bonchurch, while the great down above is simply called St Boniface. Monks from Lyra in Normandy are said to have built a church here, hence the cove below is called Monks Bay.

The French raided Bonchurch from the sea but their leader was killed and they withdrew: King Charles paid it a visit in his early days at Carisbrooke Castle, but for hundreds of years the village remained an isolated community of fishermen and farmers, its only industry the quarrying of stone.

The only way into the village was by Shepherds Lane, which descended from the west to the church, fringed on one side by thatched cottages and on the other by a withy bed which provided the material for crab and lobster pots: a steep footpath led up to Cowleaze, the hill above Shanklin, and a track to the quarries above the village. All the land belonged to four farms, Luccombe, a hamlet east of the village, Macketts, Bonchurch and Marepool.

Barbara Softly's novel *A Stone in a Pool* published in 1964, set at the time of King Charles's imprisonment at Carisbrooke, alternates between the Castle and Macketts Farm: while intended for older children it paints a detailed and interesting picture of seventeenth-century Bonchurch.

But the nineteenth century was to change the neighbourhood for ever. (A print of 1821 shows Ventnor as a mill and seven cottages.) Today Shepherds Lane is a tarmac road leading up past a "new" church to The Pitts and Upper Bonchurch, or down to the shore. The great inner cliff with St Boniface towering above, the bowery trees and huge fallen rocks, all these remain, but the land between is covered by the grand houses and their spacious grounds which grew up in the 1840s, many of them through the influence of the Reverend James White.

This happened in two ways: with his wife Rosa he had come to own half the village and after some legal wrangling and a bill in parliament, let the land off in building plots: he was also a man of culture, an historian and contributor to *Punch Magazine*. He had a house called Wood Lynch built for himself. Friendly and hospitable he invited his literary friends to stay and this resulted in an influx of famous names: here Tennyson's favourite black felt hat was seized upon by his young lady admirers and cut up into souvenir pieces!

For most local people the name Bonchurch immediately conjures up "the pond" and a wander round its quiet lanes and steps must start there in the village street. Early in the nineteenth century, Joseph Hadfield turned the withy bed or willow swamp into a small lake. It lies all along one side of the street, hung with willows, chestnut and beech trees, fringed with bamboo and laurels, home for much-fed mallard and moorhens. Opposite are a few stone cottages and a working blacksmith's. Further along a fountain stands in a small chapel-like building not unlike St

Lawrence Well, and close by a pyramid is set into the wall, inscribed "This pyramid of stone was erected in 1773 and is a sample of stone quarried in the vicinity. This stone was at that time shipped from Bonchurch for use at Portsmouth Harbour."

A drive winds up to Peacock Vane, originally called Upper Mount and opposite another leads to Under Mount: this actually passes through a dark tunnel, its walls ornamented with shells, flints and antlers, the house being built on the site of Bonchurch Farm.

Now a lane turns off towards the sea and one of the most striking of all the Victorian houses, the drum tower entrance to East Dene, built about 1826 and famous as the childhood home of Algernon Swinburne. Among the rocks of Monks Bay below he first learnt to swim and exult in the power of the sea, which was to surge through his poems long after he had left the island.

Just below, at Winterbourne, Dickens came to stay in 1849 during the summer when he was writing *David Copperfield,* though he found time to climb the downs every day, take a shower bath under the waterfall and enjoy splendid literary parties at his friend James White's house, Woodlynch, with Leech, the famous *Punch* cartoonist, and Thackeray, among others. "From the top of the highest downs," he wrote, "there are views which are only equalled on the Genoese shore of the Mediterranean, the variety of walks is extraordinary," but by the autumn the Undercliff's mild climate had brought on a fit of depression, and he was complaining of a terrible languor.

In his book *Dickens on an Island,* Richard Hutchings discusses the fascinating tradition that the story of *Great Expectations* first germinated in Dickens's mind from a Bonchurch seed—a jilted woman who kept her wedding breakfast intact, perhaps the original Miss Haversham: certainly the name of Mr Dick in *David Copperfield* was borrowed from Bonchurch.

The lane leads down towards the cliffs and the Old Church: a notice proudly states "Rebuilt 1070". A little larger than St Lawrence, it shares its austere beauty within, though once the walls were painted: the most striking feature is a great black cross on the altar, seventeenth-century Flemish work brought from a Norman abbey. Outside, old gravestones lean towards the sea among roses and myrtle and ivy.

Clearly Bonchurch and St Lawrence have followed a similar

pattern of development. After all the new building of the 1840s and consequent rise in population, the little church was found inadequate, so a new one was built higher up, the land provided by the White and Swinburne families. In summer, Evensong is held every Sunday in the Old Church, by candlelight, when it is often packed to the door.

The "new" church stands in an undulating rock-strewn hollow so that the roof of an ornate mausoleum echoes the shape of a natural outcrop beside it, and some graves lie higher than the church roof, all bowered in fuchsia, yew and overhung with mature trees. Swinburne's grave is by the path with others of his family.

Inside there is a striking triple window of deep gem colours above the altar and a profusion of needlework, including a beautiful tapestry wall panel of the seasons.

Just above is the entrance to Cliff Dene, the house until 1951 of H. de Vere Stacpoole the writer, whose most famous book, *The Blue Lagoon*, reached a new public when it was filmed. The grounds extended down to the pond which he gave to the village in memory of his wife. He loved Cliff Dene dearly and wrote a delightful collection called *In a Bonchurch Garden*, describing it.

"There are others who work unpaid in this old Victorian wilderness of a garden that seems to me . . . sometimes haunted in sub tropical noons of summer by Victorian shades; gentlemen in shepherd's plaid trousers and with whiskers, ladies with parasols leading children wearing pantalettes . . . long gone garden lovers." After H. de Vere Stacpoole's death, the garden was neglected and became an overgrown jungle, but now it is being lovingly restored, terrace by terrace.

Just above, a quiet road called The Pitts, once the site of the quarries, terraces along beneath the towering inner cliff, lined with characterful Victorian houses, their grounds bounded by many stone walls delightfully characteristic of this stone country and draped with a rich variety of plants, bell flowers and lavender, valerian, stonecrop and wild sweet pea.

Here at Ashcliff, now let into flats, lived the Sewell family. Elizabeth was well known as a writer of Christian novels, kept a school at the house and helped found the village school. Her journals are full of Bonchurch cameos such as: "A walk last evening, when it was getting dark on the shore, over the wet sands and shingle to a beautiful smooth piece of sand between Bonchurch and Ventnor. It was dreamy and sad with the tide low and the white cliffs standing out in a ghost like manner and the dark seaweed covered rocks forming a background."

The Pitts peters out into a characteristic footpath—narrow between stone walls then plunging down steep steps back to the main road, near to Madeira Hall, now a hotel, where Thomas Macaulay stayed in 1850. According to his letters, he did not associate with the literary gatherings at the Whites', but delighted in solitude. "I rise before seven; breakfast at nine; write a page; ramble five or six hours over rocks and through copsewood with Plutarch in my hand; come home; write another page; take Fra Paulo and sit in the garden reading till the sun sinks behind the Undercliff." He was working at that time on his vast *History of England*.

Near the Shore Road corner at Under Rock lived Edmund Peel, a minor poet known for his poem of Wight, "The Fair Island", which includes a description of Dickens climbing the downs. Residents say the village is haunted by a ghostly passing still, which cannot be a smugglers' ruse: little wonder if some of its shades return to a village so beloved. Other famous writers were Carlisle, Keats, Karl Marx and Longfellow.

Shore Road winds steeply down under rocks and trees to Horseshoe Bay. There are some new houses and a contemporary holiday centre in a real suntrap position on the cliff top, but the luxuriant greenery soon folds them into the landscape. A small car park above syphons off traffic; in the little bay below a handful of stone houses confront the sea across a sea wall. At Bonchurch Pottery, a workshop-cum-showroom, the potter can be watched at work.

Past the terrace, mostly guesthouses, the eastern shore is a rocky wilderness strewn with chunks of ruined sea wall while to the west a vast new scheme of coastal defence is underway. In summer Horseshoe Bay is a delightfully secluded place for sampling local crabs, but in winter the small front is strewn with pebbles and seaweed, and often flooded as waves hurl against the wall. A footpath winds up behind the houses, past a pretty cascade, through old woods back to the Old Church and village.

No one should leave Bonchurch without sampling its cuisine. Winterbourne, now a hotel with many recommendations including some from Egon Ronay and Ashley Courteney, has a special Copperfield Room commemorating Dickens's stay. Peacock Vane above the village street, a white Regency house, opened its restaurant in 1955 and soon became famous for dishes which brought together the best of French, Dutch and English cooking. A recipe book printed locally was taken up by a London publisher, since when *The Peacock Vane Cookery Book—Recipes to Relish* has become a national success, every page a facsimile of Joan Wolfendon's handwriting and delightful water-colour illustrations.

One can reach Shanklin by the road over Cowleaze with its spectacular view of Sandown Bay, or walk through the romantic rock-strewn jungle of the Landslip along narrow paths originally trodden out by the feet of revenue offers on their beat watching for smugglers, and later by the coastguards. Either way will lead to the village church of St Blasius, in a lovely setting beneath the downs beside the vast spread of the green, with a willow-fringed pond full of moorhens and mallard by its gate.

Footpaths lead up to the downs, one of the best wandering over to Wroxall with splendid views along the coast and inviting side paths. The Bronze Age burial mounds up here were long ago pillaged. Sir John Oglander writes of them with dreadful casualness. "I have digged for my experience in some of ye more ancient and have found many bones of men formerly consumed by fire, for in ancient times they did desire to be buried—as near heaven as they could; dig and you shall find their bones."

Though the Undercliff adds greatly to the variety of island countryside, it is true to say that some people find it oppressive. Dickens himself finally complained of it. But at Shanklin the downs have moved back as it were, the country feels spacious and airy. In the Domesday Survey the village was called Seneliz, when it belonged to the Fitz Azor family: later it was partly owned by the de Lisles who built the original church, a memorial chapel dedicated to St Blasius, the patron saint of woolcombers.

From the road it appears L-shaped, but it is actually cruciform with a conical bell turret above the intersection: this shape dates from 1852, when it was so enlarged and restored as to be almost a new church.

Up the lane by the pond stands the manor house, now a hotel, once a secret rendezvous for island Jacobites meeting to toast "the King over the water", Prince Charles. The house met a similar fate to the church, being much altered and enlarged in 1885. Its old drive, now a sunken road with deep ferny banks overhung by oak and beech, leads into the village street.

Today Shanklin Old Village merges into its big brother resort of Shanklin town, just as Bonchurch does with Ventnor, but there the resemblance ends. The Old Village is far more sophisticated and busy, totally dedicated to the tourist trade in the same way as Godshill and similarly picturesque in a rather studied way, the narrow winding street lined with quaint thatched cottages, most of them shops, cafés or hotels and not all as old as they might at first appear—even the kiosk selling ices and postcards is thatched! But it all adds up to a busy, pretty scene in the season.

Like Bonchurch, Shanklin was for hundreds of years a small agricultural community: because of the steep cliffs it relied less on fishing than the Undercliff villages. It has been suggested that the French Revolution gave the first impetus to a native tourist trade; with France out of bounds one had to look nearer home. In 1800 there were no houses on the shore, the chine was a pathless cleft which boys sometimes scrambled down to catch eels, the only shop was a cottage selling groceries and bread, the road west was a rutted cart track up dangerously steep Cowleaze, while the road east to Lake had seven gates across it. A road led round from the brewery to the Crab Inn and there stopped, only a footpath leading across the green, or Great Mead, to the church.

Smugglers used the beach to land cargoes of spirit, French brocade, lace and tobacco, moving them inland through a tunnel in the chine, or at Luccombe further west. By 1817 there were several lodging houses in the village, so William Colenutt had a pathway made down through the chine to the shore, where he built Fisherman's Cottage. When John Keats came to stay two years later, he lodged at Eglantine Cottage in what is now Pomona Road. "Our window looks over house tops and cliffs on to the sea, so that when the Ships sail past the cottage chimneys you may take them for weathercocks. We have Hill and Dale, forest and Mead and plenty of lobsters."

Of course the path proved a boon to another kind of "visitor". A local man remembering the 1820s wrote, "We remember witnessing on a Sunday afternoon in open daylight, forty or fifty men coming from the shore and passing our dwelling in procession, each of them carrying two kegs of contraband spirits across their shoulders." Later the crew of an excise cutter were stationed in the village at Jessamine Cottage.

When a new road was made, connecting the village street to the church, more cottages and some large houses in their own grounds followed, including Pomona and Daish's Hotel. The fashion for the *cottage orné*, and the care of the White Popham family in leasing the land, resulted in a harmonious development of pretty thatched cottages with fancy carved barge-boards, such as Vernon Cottage, or houses in large landscaped grounds, Upper Chine and Westhill for example. Vine Cottage housed a general shop and a fire engine called Nil Desperandum. A guide claimed it "the loveliest village in the Isle of Wight, celebrated for its retired cottages beautifully adorned with roses, honeysuckles and flowering shrubs. Nearly every cottage was in the habit of letting lodgings: such was its Utopian happiness that the inhabitants were like one large family . . . every addition was in perfect harmony with the surrounding scenery".

But a different kind of development was taking place to the east, with the growth of a purpose-built resort, fashionable Shanklin; its station opened in 1864, and the local paper published weekly lists of important visitors arriving.

The American poet Henry Longfellow came in 1868, but he had the good fortune to stay in the Old Village, in one of its oldest buildings in fact, Holliers Hotel, originally a coaching inn, "a lovely thatched roof hotel all covered with ivy and extremely desirable. Our windows look down on the quaintest little village you ever saw. It is all like a scene on a stage".

Dickens visited Shanklin while staying at Bonchurch, for one of his funniest chapters, the honeymoon in *Our Mutual Friend*, is set on the shore.

The development of Shanklin town has meant that the Old Village has largely escaped unsightly modern development. With its wealth of trees and gardens it is still a delightful village to explore, and in summer especially a piquant mixture of old and new.

Inland, Keats's lodging in Pomona Road is entirely altered from his time, but the Wine Lodge nearby is an interesting building, retaining second-storey sack doors and low ceilings from the time when it was Shanklin Brewery, making Battleship Ale. The road down to the village street passes the Old Church Parish Room, with the classical façade of a Greek temple.

On one side of the village street stands typical early nineteenth-century Vernon Cottage, quaint angled thatch, part half-timbered, part slate hung, while on the other, at the Rock Shop, one can attend demonstrations of how the letters get into the rock. The Crab Inn, three hundred years old, full of old prints and low beams, naturally specializes in seafood salads; Daish's and Holliers both run casinos, Pencil Cottage sells souvenirs, mugs from Dunoon and crystal from West Germany; Henry VIII's Lodge has court menus—Cardinal Wolsey is deep-fried scampi. Everywhere cabaret, hot dogs and beach hats sprout beneath the thatch and roses.

But along the cliffs are quiet leafy roads, Rylstone Gardens, Keats Green, lanes to the Landslip and above all, the Chine, celebrated by Longfellow's verse. Though there are seats and steps, nothing has been done to tame its wilderness. The waterfall plunges forty feet down sheer dark cliffs, the path winding along and over the stream; below is a green twilight under tall sycamore, alder and beech, the lower slopes clothed in rhododendrons, bamboo and hydrangeas. The air is so moisture laden that all the lower rocks are greened over with carpets of liverwort, mosses and ferns.

Quiet leafy roads lead round from the chine entrance back to St Blasius. Old walls, mature trees—one might be back in Victorian Shanklin until suddenly here is a sharp-angled flat-roofed building, strictly late twentieth century, the Margaret Pasmore Theatre recently built by Upper Chine School, a reminder that this may be the Old Village but it still moves with the times.

7

The Road through the Hills

It is a stimulating contrast to move from the lush, sheltered Undercliff to the bare and windswept downlands of the south and west. The villages of Chillerton and Gatcombe lie in different valleys, yet join at a right angle to share the church. Gatcombe is a secret place, hidden deep in a fold of the downs, its few old cottages and farms strung along a lane going nowhere, while Chillerton straggles along the main road to Chale, close under the wall-like flank of Chillerton Down.

At first glance it seems the newer village, because it includes a number of modern houses and bungalows, but it did appear in Domesday, as Celertune. By the seventeenth century, though, it seems to have lost its manorial rights and to have survived only as Chillerton Farm. However, traces of the most ancient settlements are not down in the valley but on the hilltop.

A footpath provides a short cut from Chillerton to Gatcombe; from it branches another leading through farmlands, the banks bright with vetches and scabious in their season. Not a house in sight, only a flock of wood pigeons flying over, a pheasant cock-cocking in alarm, till the path turns up the steep slope of Tolt, clothed with hanging woods of beech and huge old ash trees hung with lianas of old man's beard. On the summit, bare turf, larks rising and the little chalk-loving flowers—eyebright and thyme. Various uncommon orchids grow about these hills: if you find butterfly or bee, please leave them to grow and increase: some orchid plants must live for fifteen years before producing a flower. Seven-foot teasels line the hedge. Over on the left are turf banks immediately suggesting prehistoric barrows, and they are worth scrambling up for the panoramic view from the summit over north Wight. A ventilation pipe sticking out of the top reveals that this is nothing older than Chillerton Reservoir!

But a walk southward along the broad ridge of down leads to the Five Barrows, a humpy earthwork stretching partly across the flat top. In fact it is an unfinished Iron Age fort, 275 feet long and possibly owing its shape to five gangs of workers each piling up earth. When finished it would have been levelled and topped with a wooden rampart. It is tempting to visualize the broad down top behind as a thriving Iron Age community, the first Chillerton, its people busy tilling the ground, shepherding, weaving cloth, repairing stockades round huts and stockyards and fashioning cooking pots.

Though there are lynchets or banks which still show the outlines of Celtic fields, no other evidence has yet been found of Iron Age occupation and the ramparts await expert excavation. Why were they built? There were Iron Age settlements along the Undercliff, and at Knighton near Newchurch. Was this a tribal centre where all met to build a place of refuge? It is dated between 300 B.C. and A.D. 100, and commands a splendid wide view of south-west Wight and the English Channel. Perhaps fear of a Roman invasion raised these banks. Historians consider it the forerunner of Carisbrooke Castle, as a central refuge for the people of the island.

Below, Gatcombe is honeycombed with lanes. The name of Trousers, where there were once quarries, is explained by its forked shape. The most important has always been Dark Lanes which leads in a very straight line to the back of Carisbrooke Castle and is locally believed to be a Roman road, though historians maintain there is no actual proof that the Romans built roads on the island. Certainly Dark Lanes is very old: tradition says that stone from the quarries was passed from hand to hand along a human chain stretching to Carisbrooke for the building of the castle in the eleventh century, each man being paid a penny a week.

By the thirteenth century the manor belonged to the de Estur family. At this period the island was frequently harried by the French and another tradition is that when the French penetrated as far as Garstons and camped there, the locals, having heard they were to attack the castle, waited in ambush either side of Dark Lane that night and slew every one of the enemy. The French did lay siege to the castle in 1377, invading from the north, but this may be an earlier skirmish.

When the estate was split up, some twenty years before, Joan Lisle's dowry comprised part of the hall, one third of the issue of the dovecotes and fish ponds and one third "of a plot within the court where the houses were lately burned", which may refer to the French raid. The most direct way from Chillerton to Gatcombe church is a lane passing two fields called Long Butts and Short Butts where archery was practised: in Edward III's time three bowmen were furnished to the local force.

Village tradition maintains that the original "big house" of Gatcombe, obviously an extensive range of buildings even in the fourteenth century, was built further west at the head of the valley, and that the cottage at the junction of Snowdrop and Newbarn lanes is the site of its stables, though there seems to be no documentary proof of this and it would have been a long way from the church.

In the reign of Mary Tudor, the rector Lamber Peche was forced to resign: after the Queen's death he tried to return, but one William Clifford refused to give up the living, though he "suffered the chancel of the same to fall to the ground for lack of repairing of the same".

By the seventeenth century Gatcombe belonged to the Worsley family. In 1637 the churchwardens petitioned for a rate to be raised for repairs to the church "fallen into decay". The rate was granted, but John Worsley who owned half the land and had moreover taken possession of the church house refused to pay it!

A later Worsley, Sir Edward, was one of the chief agents of

King Charles I while he was imprisoned in Carisbrooke Castle. After the failure of the first rescue attempt, a second plan was devised which involved Sir Edward and others waiting on horseback below the castle walls, ready to spirit the King away to a ship on the north coast, but this plot was betrayed and the riders fired on. Sir Edward escaped to Holland, but later was allowed to return to Gatcombe on payment of a fine of three pounds, six shillings and eightpence to the Commonwealth.

The present Gatcombe House was built by the Worsleys in 1750, near the ancient church, so it does seem likely they rebuilt on the old site. At that time the road from Chale passed behind Sheat Manor and straight on across the front of Gatcombe House to emerge near the church. In the 1820s, Squire Campbell took a dislike to this arrangement and so the road was re-routed round the present sharp corners, from Chillerton.

Gatcombe, which seems so timeless, has seen similar changes. The old road from Newport led up to Hill Farm, then turned down across what was then the park to the church, but a Doctor Lowe, squire at that time, took exception to the peasantry tramping across his land so built the steep detour now known as Doctor's Shute. The old way is still visible as a line of trees: the farmer retained the right to walk down it on Sundays, while the rector had a coffin right of way.

Snowdrop Lane and Hollow Lane are both beautiful shady walks on a hot day, green tunnels with deep mossy banks draped with ivy and fern, full of secret refuges for wood mice, bank voles and nesting wrens. In the nineteenth century, though, there were cottages in Snowdrop Lane, another farm at its entrance, and what is now a dairy holding was the school for both villages, until the present school was built in Chillerton. The cottages near Sheat Manor were the blacksmith's shop, and the mill lay hidden in the Medina valley eastwards.

A large pond at the bottom of Snowdrop Lane was turned into a water source for the village—the pump has gone but Pond Cottage remains. The Seely family who owned large island estates were responsible for the pump and also the slate-roofed cottages designed by Miss Seely on the lines of Durham miners' cottages. Every tenant received a ton of coal for the winter and a Christmas dinner.

The medieval strip system of farming lingered on here—the

common lands round Hollow Lane were not enclosed till the mid nineteenth century, while even today, the parish half acre is a narrow strip bordered by two others belonging to different farms. Small Gains is still a rubbishy little field, while the name Kingsbrooms Field remains an interesting puzzle. Gallants Lane, on high ground towards Carisbrooke, is said to derive from the view—the top gallants or masts of ships in the Solent could be seen from its highest point. A lane leading towards Rookley was originally called Jacobs Stocks; in the local tongue this became Jackie Stalks.

Today a walk round Gatcombe can include Gatcombe Park, for it has recently been opened to the public. An avenue of limes leads up to the house, an austere square building best seen in autumn when its mantle of Virginia creeper glows scarlet. Acres of green parkland include a lake fringed with reeds, and sedge, while overhanging beech and sycamore provide tunnels of cover for coot and ducks. A woodland walk turns off along the stream by banks of ferns, all green and peaceful with only the drumming of a woodpecker and flicker of dragon-flies to disturb the air. Benches invite one to picnic by the lake, or simply bird-watch.

But in another part of the grounds a different kind of pool displays radio-controlled model boats, with a children's playground nearby.

Inside, there is a museum of cameras and typewriters for the specialist, but the main exhibition is a complete collection of Brannon prints of the Isle of Wight. George Brannon came here from Ireland in 1810. The pictures were originally drawn, engraved and published as illustrations to *Vectis Scenery*, first brought out in 1822 by George, Alfred and Philip Brannon. The style can best be described as awe-inspiring, every down a mountain and every valley a dark chasm, but endlessly interesting as records of nineteenth-century Wight—the village of Upper Ryde, for example. The one of Gatcombe House itself illustrates artistic licence at its height, showing a yacht in full sail on the lake, with a tiny house in the distance. Actually there were plans to flood the marsh and form a real lake, but these were never realized.

Upstairs, each bedroom has had a wall removed and replaced by glass to display tableaux of costume through the ages against a period background, most of the clothes having come from the

Monte Carlo Opera—and they are beautiful, the whole idea carried out with great attention to detail and most elegantly arranged. The Victorian drawing-room scene, for example, includes lustre vases on the mantelpiece, little reticules for the ladies, music of the period on the piano.

Gatcombe Park is one of the latest holiday attractions: its displays are unique on the island and one could well spend a whole day there—it really deserves to succeed. Near the pond a small gate leads through into Gatcombe churchyard and the grey stone church built in the thirteenth century as a manorial chapel by the Estur family. The tower added in the fifteenth century is girdled by curious gargoyles, another of which surmounts the porch—only added in 1910 but so cunningly it appears as ancient as the rest.

The little church is full of interest; a carpet runner striped in jewel colours echoes the brilliance of Pre-Raphaelite stained-glass windows in the sanctuary; while fifteenth-century glass depicts golden angels curiously feathered all over, with a chequer board; a full-length marble effigy of Charles Seely of Gatcombe Park, killed at Gaza in 1917, contrasts sharply with an ancient wooden one thought to be a crusading Estur—a small winged cherub guards his left ear. The choir stalls were carved from oaks felled in Gatcombe Park—yet one more feudal touch.

Rabbits help mow the grass outside: the churchyard is tucked away out of this world, shaded by great trees, full of flowers in their season. Outside the lane runs westward between sheltering hills, past a few old cottages and finally peters out into farm roads. Here half-way up a southerly slope stand the kennels of the Isle of Wight Hunt. At the top of the bank the original kennel buildings, built in 1920, have begun to slip and have been abandoned: below them in a large sunny field yard, forty couples of foxhounds spend their time off, galloping as one to the wire netting at any sign of entertainment such as a passer-by, with salvos of amiable barks, and high tails wagging.

They are divided into a dog and bitch pack, working alternate hunts, sleeping in their separate lodges in the newer range of buildings below. On non-hunting days they get an early morning walk round the lanes or up on the down, ideal dog country away from roads, then their feed, raw meat from casualty carcasses, then a siesta in their field and another run in the afternoon. Pups are bred in spring and trained up during the non-hunting summer season, each coupled up to an experienced hound.

Though foxes have not yet taken to town dwelling on the island, they are very common, strolling about in daylight in the country and visiting Carisbrooke village by night. But the Gatcombe fox excels them all in sheer cheek. In the spring a hen made a nest in the hounds' enclosure and laid thirteen eggs. Under the noses of eighty hounds, a fox killed the hen and ate eleven eggs, leaving only the two afterwards found to be bad!

Returning to the main road through Chillerton, this turns a sharp bend by Sheat Manor, which presents to the passer-by a fine E-shaped south front with tall stone gables at either end. It was built by the Urry family and adorned with fine carved Jacobean panelling, but this was stripped out and sold to America before the last war.

On the next corner a stream appears briefly. As in Niton, this once flowed all the way down beside the village street but is now banished into a culvert for much of its length. Further along it reappears on the other side on a triangle of grass called The Green, from which a sunken way, Hollow Lane, leads up to the higher farmlands. Beneath it, springs rise to form the stream which was walled in here to form a sheep-wash—the walls are still there though overgrown with water weeds. Of course the downs used to be great sheep runs. Some slopes were ploughed during the last war and have remained so, others supported cattle, but in the 1980s the movement is back to sheep.

For many years there stood beside the sheep dip what could only be described as an enormous lump of ivy, inside of which stood a disused chapel. Recently this has been stripped of its green mantle, repaired and enlarged to become the village community centre, to be used particularly for young people's activities. Neither Chillerton nor Gatcombe has a pub, though Chillerton has a thriving licensed social club which largely takes its place.

As the road begins its climb over the downs it passes the fine old stone barns of Chillerton Farm, while high above towers the T.V. mast, close by the Iron Age fort. Then the road dips down Berry Shute, levelling out as it passes Billingham Manor, said to be haunted by the head of Charles I which appeared on the days when executions were carried out at Parkhurst Prison. A lane to the right leads to yet another manor, one with its own church, at the hamlet of Kingston.

Undulating farm-lands stretch away on either hand, then a sharp turn eastwards brings one to Chale—two Chales really, connected by a mile-long country road running parallel to the long ridge of St Catherine's Down. On that sharp bend stands a village pub properly called The Star, but still known to the locals as Sprake's Brewery.

This was founded by Robert Sprake in 1833. The beer was made from locally grown hops and barley and was taken round the harvest fields in buckets, so soon became popular with the locals, and later the thirty-six gallon casks were taken all over the island by wagon, there being a special contract to supply the stations: the excise duty on a cask in the 1830s was sixpence. A boy of small stature was always employed in the brewery so that he could get down into the vats to clean them out.

Today The Star is a low-beamed, comfortable pub with hot and cold snacks always on offer: the front half of the bar represents the complete ground floor of the original seventeenth-century cottage, while a spacious children's room behind is the old beer store with a trapdoor in the ceiling leading up to the brewery floor where one door is still labelled Fermenting Room. In the bar there is a framed label: even in 1833 it was called Ye Olde Home Brewed Ale, while the well which supplied the brewery is now under the kitchen floor.

Chale Green is a straggle of houses round a wide grassy space lately rolled and reseeded, enclosed till 1855. In 1870 there lived around the green a shoeing smith, wheelwright and carpenter, a sweep, a beer retailer, a grocer and shoemaker. Today there is a general store and petrol pump, the beer retailer or New Inn having closed. Until recently the buildings included a few old stone cottages with a mix of Victorian and a few modern houses, the general impression being of a working farming community: nineteenth-century records show the farms specialized in early lambs, dairy herds and barley.

But now the western side of the green has been taken over by a large new housing project, nearly sixty dwellings, some of them flats, some short terraces of houses in buff brick, an unusual development, because all the houses are to rent. This kind of accommodation is very short on the island where holidaymakers will pay higher summer rents than those resident all year, so what lets there are tend to be only short winter ones. The estate has brought concrete pavements and street lighting to the village, though the green itself has been extended. Perhaps the growth of gardens and trees will help it settle into the landscape.

High under the down's northern edge lies one of the manors of Chale, Gotten, or originally Godeton, now a stone and slate farm house. Before the Normans came, the manor belonged to Bruning and his brother, but really enters history in the fourteenth century when a ship called the *St Mary of Bayonne* laden with casks of wine was wrecked on the rocks of Atherfield Ledge in Chale Bay. The wine was seized as wreck of the sea "by divers men of the country" and fifty-three barrels came into the possession of Walter de Godeton. He and others were then taken to court and sued for the value of the wine.

The matter would have ended there, had the wine not belonged to a monastery in Picardy. Godeton was further charged with sacrilege and ordered, as a token of remorse, to build a lighthouse and maintain a chantry priest to say Masses and keep the light. So an oratory was built on the summit of St Catherine's Down overlooking the scene of the shipwreck (though old records suggest that one stood there already). While the chapel walls have disappeared, the strong little lighthouse remains, thirty-six feet high, with a pointed roof and massive octagonal lantern, where long ago Walter de Langeberewe tended a furze fire every night, to shine out through the slits in the stonework and warn ships at sea to keep away from the terrible rocks below.

Nearby is the site of one of the alarm beacons kept ready to light in the times of invasion scares, but lit more recently on the happy occasion of Prince Charles's wedding as a link in the chain of beacons lit across Britain. Also close by stands the ruin of another lighthouse, begun in 1830 but abandoned because it was frequently obscured by low clouds. Its place was taken by the present lighthouse on the low cliffs at Niton. The slim tower of the oratory and the low bowl of the old lighthouse are often referred to locally as the Pepper and Salt Pots.

A fine ridge walk leads northwards to another hill monument, the Hoy Pillar, over seventy feet high, surmounted by a stone ball. This was erected by one Michael Hoy, in 1814, to

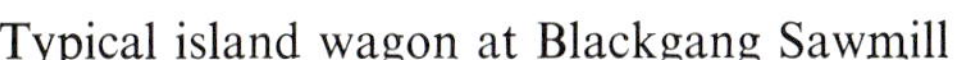

Working steam engine at the sawmill, Blackgang Chine

Typical island wagon at Blackgang Sawmill

Entrance to Carisbrooke Castle

Carisbrooke Church

Westover Manor, Calbourne

Westover Manor, an interior

Calbourne Water Mill

Once the track to the Lifeboat House, Brooke cliffs

Entrance to Mottistone Manor

Shate, Brighstone

Water meadows, Brighstone

Cottages at Shorwell

Westcourt Manor, Shorwell

Woolverton Manor, Shorwell

commemorate the visit of the Emperor of Russia, Alexander I, the stone being dressed in the barn of Gotten Farm below. According to the then landlord of The Star, Oscar Sprake, one of his customers once took a dare and stood on his head on the top of the stone ball—Sprake's ale must have been pretty strong!

Michael Hoy had lived for many years in Russia, then became owner of a house sheltering beneath the northern summit of St Catherine's called on a map of 1775 The Hermitage, evidently after The Oratory, but later deeds also refer to it as Armitage. Was that the original name, or simply a typical island broadening of vowels? In 1844 the house was leased to Henry Dawes, late of Her Majesty's 22nd Regiment, who evidently felt a certain bitterness that his land should include a stone tribute to the Russian Emperor, and to redress the balance, had an inscription placed on the opposite side of the pillar base, "In honour of those brave men of the Allied Armies who fell on the Alma at Inkermann and at the Siege of Sebastopol, 1857."

The present Hermitage was built in 1895, a substantial stone house with thirteen bedrooms and spacious living-rooms: nevertheless by 1971 it was badly dilapidated, the ground floor used as a grain store and the seventeenth-century coach house turned into a milking parlour. Today it is a comfortable and elegant conference centre, miles even from a village, bowered in rhododendrons with a lovely view right across the little humpy hills of south-east Wight to Sandown Bay. The Admiral's Cup team stayed here in Cowes Week, apparently undisturbed by She, a female presence said to haunt one of the bedrooms, announcing her presence by a violet fragrance. Elizabeth Sewell, the Victorian novelist who lived in the Undercliff, wrote a novel called *Ursula*, set in The Hermitage.

The oldest part of Chale stands near the windswept southern cliffs. Chale Farm, one of three Domesday manors, with Gotten and Walpen, is one of the oldest houses on the island, a fourteenth-century hall with Tudor additions (though much remodelled inside) built by John de Langford, Constable of Carisbrooke Castle and Warden of Wight. Beside it stands a fine barn of the same period. The house is often referred to as Chale Abbey, in books and even maps, but has no monastic connections: the name presumably sprang up from the church-like shape of the east window: as a further corruption, it was also known as Chale Anney.

The church school, built in 1843, is still in use: opposite stands the rugged grey church of St Andrew, its tower having withstood five centuries of south-westerly gales sweeping up the Channel from the Atlantic. It was begun in 1114 for the manor tenants; now the outside is largely Perpendicular in style. The pulpit, carved by a local woman in 1866, has a fine front panel depicting Jesus preaching to his disciples, while the altar is surmounted by four tall gilded angels. Of various brightly coloured Victorian stained-glass windows the most unusual, dedicated to W. Jacobs, shows Jacob asleep dreaming of the ladder of angels ascending into heaven.

From the churchyard can be seen cliffs and headlands of this cruel, beautiful coast stretching away to the Needles: in stormy weather the air resounds with a deep growling thunder of waves crashing on the steep shore and sucking back shingle in their deadly undertow. The church registers are full of melancholy entries recording the burials of drowned sailors.

For example, "1832, Master, seaman and boy of the Brig Crosique wrecked in Chale Bay. Adolf Wall, captain of Swedish Galliot Charles II of one hundred tons burden, laden with fruit which was wrecked off the Sandrock Spring Dispensary early on morning of Christmas Day 1832. John Acksell Wall, son of the above, ditto Sturman Gustaff Linbon mate of the above galliot, which struck and immediately went to pieces." (A galliot was a small cargo boat.)

The northern end of the churchyard has many seamen's graves including eighteen from one ship, *The Clarendon*. Nearer the road, the large box tombs were used to hide smuggled brandy and even the smugglers themselves if the excise men were too hot on their trail.

Next door stands the pub, originally called The White Mouse.

The Clarendon, with twenty-seven people aboard and a cargo of sugar and rum, was wrecked below Blackgang in 1836. George Brannon wrote, "The ship, rapidly driven by the raging elements, was soon aground, engulphed between the mountain waves . . . for about five minutes were heard the convulsive screams of the unhappy sufferers, but 'ere any measure could be taken for their escape, the ship was stove in by one tremendous surge wrenching the hull asunder into a thousand pieces—all on board perished." In fact one of the fishing family of Wheelers had run right along the cliffs from Chale, summoning help as he went and bravely rescued three of the crew.

Much timber was thrown ashore and some of it used to enlarge the inn which was renamed The Clarendon. Now, however, the wheel has come full circle; its extension has been christened The White Mouse. This is an Egon Ronay pub.

A shipwreck fund was set up in 1849 with an annual income of nine guineas, to supply clothes and comforts to those wrecked on the coast between St Catherine's Point and Freshwater.

Walpen, originally a separate manor from Chale, lies west of the church along the Military Road facing the sea. A small farmhouse, originally of wattle and daub, it was left empty in 1968 but eventually saved from ruin by a loving restoration, stones from an old brew house being used to build a new wing.

Opposite, the cliffs stretch away treeless and bare, westward, broken only by a series of chines. Chale is an odd village, by the sea but cut off from it by the pathless cliff face. The nearest break is Walpen Chine but even this provides no way to the shore. A narrow bare cleft runs parallel with the cliff edge, then turns a sharp corner and spills its stream over the sheer edge of the cliff. Its orange-brown walls are pitted with rabbit holes, a haunt of jackdaws and foxes. The records of Walpen manor show that at one time it owned a windmill and a water mill, so presumably this stream must once have been harnessed to turn a wheel.

Before the cutting of Blythe Shute, the old way to Blackgang went almost straight across by the church and continued along the lane called The Terrace. A path to the right led round to a sandpit and some fisherman's cottages, while the lane turned left along the cliffs, passed right across Blackgang Chine and regained the old road near a house called Southview, but the whole of this stretch, the cottages and several of the substantial stone houses of The Terrace itself have long perished in cliff falls.

When the new road, from Chale to Blackgang and Niton, was being excavated in 1932, a vigilant local man noticed a small shard of pottery sticking out of the bank. (This road, of necessity much further inland, cuts into the southern shoulder of St Catherine's Down.) Below, the bank showed a black stripe. On excavation this proved to be the ashes on the hearth of a Bronze Age hut. As the road work went on, traces of other huts were found.

So here in a hollow of the down and near a spring, about three thousand years ago stood a little village, made of round thatched huts with conical roofs supported on a centre pole; the people used flint scrapers to dress the skins of their oxen and sheep, hammer stones to split bones. Higher up the down is a burial mound where a cairn of beach pebbles cover the bones, and each one must have been carried up a steep climb of five hundred feet from a shore at that time much further south than it is now.

Local children used to be brought up on the story that Blackgang was named after a band of dreadful men who lured ships on to the rocks. An eighteenth-century writer averred: "They fix a lantern to the head of an old horse, one of whose legs had been previously tied up. The limping gait of the animal gave the lantern a kind of motion similar to a ship's light and led the deceived pilot to fall a prey to merciless plunderers." Now this is generally reckoned to be a picturesque fiction and a baseless slander against a community which, though it welcomed everything useful that floated ashore, often risked its own lives, as in the wreck of *The Clarendon*, to save the drowning.

In fact Blackgang probably means black path, for the lower cliffs are sinisterly dark, and the name originally referred to the great chine, the place growing up round it. A guide book of 1861 mentions only the hotel and bazaar and "a little village of villas springing up above Blackgang". Writers of that period—engravers too—loved a touch of Gothic horror in their picturesque views. "The Chine is a black and sombre chasm far in the depth of adamantine rocks five hundred feet high, down the bed of which dark waters flow . . . its shelving sides bare of trees and vegetation, the black crumbling soil, the shivered cliffs, the beetling precipices . . ."

Already the process of taming the chine had begun. The Dabell family first opened it to the public in 1843, the hotel and bazaar being the first attractions. Queen Victoria paid a visit: later Queen Mary would drive over, every Cowes week. Today the chine describes itself as a Fantasy Theme Park, one of the major tourist attractions in the south of England. It is important as an employer of local labour, especially in summer, and provides something for everyone, water gardens, adventure park, maze, Hell's Mouth,

Mission Control, a complete Cowboy Town from Pinewood Studios, dinosaurs, a museum—the island's answer to Disneyland in fact.

But the chine refuses to be tamed entirely. All along this stretch of coast, strata of heavy stone overlay unstable and treacherous "blue slipper" clay which oozes out when wet, leaving the rest unsupported. For a long period the annual loss of cliff due to this erosion was eight to twelve feet, but in 1979 and 1980 this grew to forty feet each year and if this frightening rate were to continue, the road itself would be cut by 1986. What is more, the force of the sea with the prevailing south-westerly wind behind it immediately starts devouring the fallen land, preventing the building up of a lower terrace, like the Undercliff round to the east.

So the latest attraction, The Sawmill Museum, has been built on the landward side of the road. Here a Victorian dwelling house has been stripped back to its origin as a barn and converted into a water mill: it brings to life the many village trades connected with wood—bodger, cooper, wheelwright, even charcoal burner. And if the chine's attractions are not to be lost to the sea, they must all eventually be moved back across the road to more stable ground, a new maze grown, new water gardens planted out. A secondary problem is shelter, for few trees will grow to maturity in the salt-laden sea winds.

Recent landslides have closed most of the old road to Niton to all except intrepid walkers. Here several houses have been demolished, others fallen and already moss and ivy, buddleia and sycamore seedlings begin to green over the ruins, reclaiming them for butterfly and fox, bee and bank vole.

8

Beneath the Downs

Carisbrooke village winds uphill through the valley of the Lukely Brook, its High Street dominated on the north by the majestic Norman church of St Mary, up on its bank, and on the south across the valley by the great ramparts and keep of the Castle—an historic and important place long before Newport became a town. But an even older village is thought to have existed a mile or so further up the brook, in the flat lands beneath Bowcombe Down.

In Domesday, a church is mentioned at Beaucombe, rather than Carisbrooke: though no trace of one remains, this is not surprising as early churches were built of wood. Even earlier the Romans settled here just above the brook. Though the Newport and Brading villas are in a better state of repair, Bowcombe valley and Clatterford show the greatest concentration of buildings.

Near Bowcombe Farm various traces of occupation have been found, including Samian pottery, a harness ring, roof tiles and window glass: half a mile further down, a villa was partially excavated in 1856 though now covered up, while at the bottom of the Vicarage garden lies a third villa which had walls of chalk faced with flints and floors of red tiles except for one room which had a mosaic floor of red, white, black and blue tesserae in geometric and floral patterns: finds included coins and jewellery. All three villas were probably modest farmhouses. Spickernel, who excavated this last, commented: "A quantity of bones scattered in the rooms, woodashes and fire marks on the pavements indicate its occupation by ruder people than its Roman masters." In other words the natives took over after the Romans departed. (The Newport villa bears similar signs.)

Certainly the Carisbrooke villa suffers rude neglect now. Plans are underway for an all-island museum to be opened at the Old Grammar School in Newport, where displays of Roman finds will make it easier to build up a picture of Bowcombe valley some seventeen hundred years ago.

According to the *Anglo-Saxon Chronicle*, the Saxon Cerdic and his son Cynric and their forces fought the natives here, and won in A.D. 530. Cerdic then gave the island to his nephews Stuf and Wihtgar, who was buried here in 544, so possibly he lived here also and the place became Wihtgarasburgh, the name Carisbrooke being derived from the last three syllables. (In 1890 another Wihtgar guarded the castle—he was a large St Bernard.)

In spite of documentary evidence of that first church in Bowcombe, local tradition says that a heathen temple stood on the site of the present St Mary's. After the Norman Conquest William Fitz Osborn presented the abbey of Lyra, in Normandy, with the church at Carisbrooke. In the next century the abbey founded a Benedictine priory on the north side, building another aisle on to the south of the church for the village people: the parish stretched from the Solent to the Channel: this included to the north of the Priory, the Hospital of St Augustine for the infirm—a Lepers' Hospital, marked on old maps as St Augustine's Gate.

Every time war flared against France, the French Benedictines were sent away—the Priory was finally suppressed in 1415; as it fell into ruin the stones were carted away to help build an adjacent farmhouse, and probably the great church tower, built in 1470. Through the Worsleys, Carisbrooke came into the hands of Sir Francis Walsingham, who pulled down the chancel of the church and put in the east window instead, paying the village one hundred marks in compensation. In the nineteenth century a gallery at the west end was removed and the building of a new chancel considered, but local opinion was against tampering with the old building. The latest repairs to the stonework used fibre glass—which sounds hideous, but is quite undetectable and will wear even longer than stone.

Today the church is a vast, light building of majestic proportions and soaring, battlemented tower with a fine peal of eight bells. Massive Norman pillars separate nave from Lady Chapel: in the north-east corner, the blocked doorway from which the monks entered the church from their dormitory stair is one of the few traces left of Carisbrooke Priory, though there is much else of interest, a stone coffin, the beautiful angel-tomb of Lady Wadham, aunt of Jane Seymour, a great slab in the floor which may have been the monks' stone altar, enigmatic drawings on the stone of an alcove, a cross jewelled with the buttons of a mess waistcoat of the Argyll and Sutherland Highlanders, church furniture from Osborne House given by Princess Beatrice—an atmosphere of ageless tranquillity.

The wide north-east extension of the graveyard was reserved for soldiers from Albany Barracks, the west end for Roman Catholics: the yew tree of massive girth is shown in a sixteenth-century drawing so is older than the oldest tombstone. Along the north wall can be traced sepulchral arches once within priory cloisters, while at the west end the arch of the parish gun alcove is still plainly seen.

The parish registers contain various footnotes to history, including two royal visits. "1609. King James landed and saw a muster at huny hill dine at the Castle and saw in afternoone most of the island with Prince Charles his sonne one the West Meadowe and hunted in the parke killed a bucke and so departed againe to bewly the 2 of August 1609 being Wednesday." Nine years later "Prince Charles landed at the cowes and came into the forest and saw a skirmish there and went from thence to Abbington [Alvington Down] and looked over the island and came to the castle".

"The forest" means Parkhurst, which stretched at one time from the River Medina to Newtown and southward to

Carisbrooke itself, while "the park" means part of Alvington Manor. The word park still occurs in several farm names. On the edge of the forest were the Lawnes (a name still used in the New Forest for open grazing land). Early in the seventeenth century John Harvey, lord of the manor of Alvington had his cattle impounded by the Crown for straying from the Lawnes into the forest. The boundary was called the Markeway, though there was neither hedge nor ditch.

For many years after the forest was thrust back northwards, the land between remained pasture. Its first slight upheaval was the coming of the railway from Newport to Freshwater, in 1889. Carisbrooke station was built north of the church, the way down to it a farm track past the pond at Priory Farm which was probably the monks' fishpond.

After the closing of the railway in 1953 the line reverted for a while to a lane, its banks a sprawl of vetches and garden flowers gone wild from the station garden, here a rose, there a sweet pea, but the building of Carisbrooke High School and later other schools opened up the whole area so that Priory Fields are now covered with new housing estates, and the old railway line in its turn has become a road.

As Newport flourished it began to send out brick tentacles westwards, which now join town and village, but at the beginning of the nineteenth century the houses between were known as New Village; this is where John Keats came to stay in 1817, at Mrs Cook's, in what is now called Castle Road, where he made himself at home. "I have unpacked my books, put them into a snug corner, pinned up Haydon, Mary Queen of Scotts and Milton with his daughters in a row. In the passage I found a head of Shakespeare—I have hung over my Books, having first discarded a french Ambassador—now this alone is a good morning's work." He meant to explore the whole island, and fell in love with the castle he could see from his window. "The trench is o'ergrown with the smoothest turf, and the Walls with ivy—The Keep within side is one Bower of ivy—a Colony of Jackdaws have been there many years. I dare say I have seen many a descendant of some old cawer who peeped through the Bars at Charles I, when he was there in Confinement."

Local tradition has it that he stood on the lower slope of Bowcombe Down, now Nodgham Lane, looked across to the castle on its green mound, and wrote the famous opening lines "A thing of beauty is a joy forever, Its loveliness increases . . ." But it tends to be forgotten that after all his settling in and future plans, Keats stayed only just over a week. He was lonely "and moreover I know not how it was—I could not get wholesome food". He remembered the island, though, with enough affection to return in 1819 when he stayed at Shanklin.

Castle Street, a narrow lane, leads from the church down to the old ford across the Lukely where there is now a footbridge (a famous spot for photographing the church with the cottages of the old village in the foreground), then a steep footpath climbing a meadow brings one to the castle moat, which never held water but whose grassy banks make a splendid circular walk. From the north side can be seen the whole of Carisbrooke, the church opposite on its low mound and the wide valley between, threaded by the little stream that used to be so important to the village.

Fifty years ago the view would have shown a chain of lakes all down the valley, for the Lukely turned the massive wheels of at least six mills before falling into the River Medina at Newport Quay.

The highest up the stream seems to have been a paper mill which is shown on a map of 1769 but which has long disappeared. It stood near the present ford at Clatterford: until a few years ago the older locals always called this field Papermills. Below the ford stretched the very large pond impounded for Kents Mill, the water meadows along it rich with marsh marigolds, or kingcups as they are called in these parts. The miller's house, and the huge ruins of the mill complex, stand at the end of Castle Street. From below that ford stretched another big pond, the water store for Priory Mill, which once stood on the site of the present waterworks; this pond remains though much reduced.

Kents Mill, one of the most prosperous on the island, could withhold water from the lower mills and there were constant squabbles between the two. In 1380 John Stonelether was murdered in Kents Mill (it was called Kings Mill at that time), possibly an early industrial dispute.

Below Priory Mill where the stream runs beside the road another vast pond fed Westmill, now at the entrance to Newport.

This is now largely reclaimed, only a small stretch of the reeds, locally called "spires", remains of what formed a real bird sanctuary in Victorian times. "Beautiful old West Mill is flanked by a great breadth of flowering reeds where swans and waterfowl breed. In September the spire bed is the evening resort of all the swallows in the island. After sunset a stream of excited birds arrive—the air is darkened with their quivering wings till they settle down to roost, twittering and fidgetting."

A sideline of all this water was a thriving watercress industry, the stream being renowned for its purity. This applied especially to a little feeder brook rising below the castle whose water, according to local tradition, begins as snow falling on the mountains of Switzerland and, melting, flows underground to Carisbrooke. It was used in folk medicine by the "white witches" or wise women of the village and even in living memory an elderly island woman taken sick in Wales sent for some "Carisbrooke water" as a certain cure.

That delightfully fanciful historian Davenport Adams wrote, "In my opinion the stream which ripples now through the valley was in Roman days of sufficient magnitude to carry their galleys even beyond the castle, perhaps as far as Clatterford." Today even rowing boats have disappeared, but the lanes below the castle, deep banked and quiet, often crossing fords or footbridge, are pleasant walking country. Herons fish above Papermills, mallards and swans still nest along the brooks and black-headed gulls squabble above the valley even though, by island standards, it is deep inland.

To the majority of visitors, though, Carisbrooke means the Castle, high on its mound, beautiful at all times but especially so in autumn when the beech woods at its foot glow into flame colours. The most famous picture of the castle is the entrance across the moat and between two imposing drum towers. This leads into a vast courtyard where steps lead up to the walk round the walls with wide views across the island, though the very best is from the top of the Keep, a further seventy-one steps up.

Within the walks stand the well house* with its famous donkey wheel, the guard house, the rebuilt chapel of St Nicholas, various walls which indicate the ruins of fourteenth-century domestic buildings, and the imposing Great Hall and Constables House, now used as a museum. Beyond lie a rose garden, grassy walls round the lower ramparts and the bowling green—Carisbrooke Castle is vast; seven acres in fact; worth a whole day's exploration.

Part of its fame is of course its connection with Charles I who was imprisoned here and twice tried to escape. The 1964 novel *Mary of Carisbrooke*, by Margaret Campbell Barnes, tells the story through the eyes of a local girl, while *The Royal Prisoner* is a factual account by the present curator, Dr Jack Jones. But the history of the castle itself is having to be rewritten in the light of recent excavations by the Department of the Environment.

It was long accepted that the castle rested on Roman foundations, but the excavations revealed the ruins of a Saxon wooden hall with a pagan burial of a woman and her grave goods including a glass bowl and a comb, probably of the sixth century. The dig went right down to the basic chalk without finding any Roman traces.

The next exciting find, in the courtyard, was an enormous ditch, an early Norman ringwork making a kidney shape round the north-eastern quarter, and all this before the building of the great keep in 1101 and the first fortifying with stone by the de Redvers in the twelfth century. Also a Saxon midden, or rubbish dump, was found, tidied away in the thirteenth-century, probably on the orders of Isabella de Fortibus, that energetic lady responsible for so much building within the walls that it became known as the New Castle of Carisbrooke, and she herself as Queen of the island. A new guide book is in hand describing all these recent finds.

The museum too is being reorganized so that the lower gallery will display the medieval history of the island and castle incorporating some of the latest evidence, while the upper gallery concentrates on later history, particularly the time of King Charles's residence, also wrecks and smuggling, the corn and wool trade and a special display of Tennyson relics. A collection of water-colours by John Nixon affords charming pictures of the island in the eighteenth century.

The largest exhibit is a model of the entire castle as it stood in 1377 when it was besieged by the French which shows further outer defences of spiked wooden stockades, small buildings inside the keep itself, timber shelters at intervals along the high ramparts and most surprising of all, the drum towers with upper half-timbered storeys surmounted by conical roofs of green slate which came from Cornwall.

Another surprising aspect is the castle as an unofficial nature reserve. One of the staff has made a study of wild flowers to be found within the outer walls in 1979 and 1980: he found 126 species, including such unusual ones as shining cranesbill, fairy flax and star of Bethlehem. Viper's bugloss grows in sky-blue spikes along the tops of the walls, rock rose casts a yellow glow over the high banks. Other rarities include green alkanet, basil thyme and three kinds of orchid including autumn lady's tresses, like tiny fragrant white gladioli.

When the last visitor has gone, at sunset, the other denizens of the castle come out: stoats and weasels go mousing along the crannied walls, the resident pair of little owls shriek to each other, the male perched on an ancient gun muzzle—and one small resident of the gatehouse flies out to take the air. Some years ago a colony of greater horseshoe bats inhabited a disused stairway in the gatehouse, but later disappeared: in 1981 one was discovered hanging from a pipe under the entrance arch and evidence of further droppings has excited hopes that a colony of this now rare animal may be re-forming.

The descendants of Keats's jackdaws still flourish, and kestrels hover above the walls. Less usual is the pair of mallard ducks who have chosen for seven years to nest in a secluded corner. When the yellow fledglings are old enough, the mother bird leads them from the nest: as soon as they appear in the courtyard, all traffic is stopped, visitors marshalled to one side, while mother duck and the ducklings in line astern proceed under the gateway, over the bridge and across the car park to the fields leading down to the stream!

With the thousands of visitors attracted to the castle each year, it is surprising at first sight that Carisbrooke is not more of a tourist village on the lines of Godshill: in fact it used to be, with Castle Street given up to tea shops and gardens, but today traffic goes straight to the castle without passing through the village, so that it has become largely a dormitory for Newport. Very recently, though, there are signs of another change: three eating houses, including an Italian restaurant, a pottery studio and antique shop now cater for the visitor.

The railway has come and gone, its most lasting influence

being on Gunville, a northern outlier of Carisbrooke and originally farm land carved out of Parkhurst Forest and the manor lands of Alvington. When the Pritchett family were looking for a more central site with a railway at hand to solve their distribution problems, they decided on Gunville and built a large brickworks there at the turn of the century, on the site of a smaller one. Red and white clay could be dug nearby. For the first time the new technology enabled them to manufacture bricks the whole year round: they invested in all the latest machinery, including a steam engine to draw wagons, and were given the brick contract for rebuilding Parkhurst Barracks—even so they had put too much money into the yard and it went bankrupt, the tall chimney remaining as a landmark for many years.

Besides being a keen archaeologist, Harry Pritchett was a fine potter. Examples of his work can be found in island homes, many of them pots obviously influenced by the shapes and scratch ornament of Bronze Age burial vessels.

The old claypits now form a large pond stocked with fish, while the brickyard site and the area nearby has become a small industrial estate of wholesale stores and cash-and-carry warehouses. Opinions as to the derivation of Gunville vary: one theory involves the siting of an actual gun, another puts forward the name of William de Gundeville, mentioned in 1292.

"The grey afternoon was wearing on to its chill close; and the steep chalky hill, leading from the ancient village, with its hoary castle and church, up over the bleak, barren down, was a weary thing to climb." So begins *The Silence of Dean Maitland*, a Victorian novel closely interwoven with the country between Carisbrooke and Calbourne—called in the story Chalkburne and Malbourne. Mary Gleed Tuttiett was the invalid daughter of a Newport doctor and often travelled with him in the trap on his country rounds: she wrote under the name Maxwell Gray.

Walkers can take the Tennyson Trail, which leads over the downs to Calbourne and beyond, part of a track from Bembridge to the Needles, said to be the oldest road on the island. The road climbs that steep hill, Alvington Shute, keeps along the north flank of Bowcombe Down—two names preserving the old manor titles—and leads to Swainston, in Calbourne parish, an historic manor house in acres of rolling parkland.

The estate is described as far back as 826 when King Egbert of

Wessex granted land to the church at Winchester, its western boundary being "along Cawelburn to the north sea". The Caul Bourn or stream which gives the village its name is now the western boundary of the whole village. In 1001 the island was subjected to yet one more Danish raid under a leader called Swein. Tradition says the Danes wintered their ships in Newtown creek, setting up a headquarters a few miles inland, hence the name Swainstone. With the more stable government of the Normans, the raids decreased and the Bishop of Winchester began the building of a hall in about 1180. Edward I came to stay for a week in 1285. By this time Swainstone had been granted a market on Wednesday and a three-day fair at the Feast of St Mary Magdalen. The house seems to have been rebuilt in the fifteenth-century but entered its heyday when it belonged to the Barringtons and their descendants, who owned the house from about 1700 to 1953. It was they who rebuilt the house in a square Georgian style.

It had become the fashion at that period to enhance the view from one's mansion—as with the building of Cook's Castle opposite Appuldurcombe—so on a slope of down visible from the windows was built the "Temple of Boreas" with a grandiose pillared portico like a Greek temple—and a little brick cottage tacked on behind!

Swainstone played a significant role in the life of Alfred Tennyson, for after he had rented Farringford at Freshwater he became close friends with Sir John Simeon (descendant of the Barringtons) and there was much visiting between the two houses. During one of their long evening talks, Sir John suggested that a poem beginning:

Oh that t'were possible
After long grief and pain
To find the arms of my true love
Round me once again . . .

really needed a prefatory poem to bring out its full meaning. From this suggestion grew the long monodrama *Maud*, a story of wild love, murder and madness, partly written at Swainstone and including one of its great trees:

Oh art thou sighing for Lebanon
In the long breeze that streams to thy delicious East

Sighing for Lebanon
Dark cedar, tho' the limbs have here increased
Upon a pastoral slope as fair
And looking to the south. . . .

On a worldly level, *Maud* was so successful financially that Tennyson was able to buy Farringford.

The Simeons gave permission for the Newport to Freshwater Railway to run through their estate, on condition they should be allotted their own private halt, so this was built at nearby Watchingwell. This was always a homely, rural line, the train being known to stop while the driver filched a rabbit for his supper, or righted a sheep stranded on its back. Perhaps the Simeons would not have given permission had they realized the line made a highway for poacher gangs, straight through from Gunville.

During the last war, German planes attacked the meadows along the railway. Where did they think they were? The morning after it was possible to walk round the fields and count dozens of black patches where incendiaries had fallen harmlessly on to the grass—but some fell on the lead roof of Swainstone and a large part of the house was gutted. However, it was skilfully restored eventually and glimpsed from the road amid its acres of green parkland and stands of fine old trees, it has every appearance of an eighteenth-century manor, while on the south side part of the ancient hall and chapel remain. It is now Swainston House Hotel and Country Club.

The Temple, though not damaged in the war, now presents a sad sight: the classical pillars still precariously stand but the cottage behind lies in ruins.

South-west, on a high slope of down behind Newbarn Farm, recent excavations have revealed a whole series of Bronze Age burials, including some in tree trunks: grave goods include some striking food pots, and the actual construction details will be full of interest when published. While the island has many barrow sites, they have suffered serious damage, some hurriedly excavated by unskilled Victorian archaeologists, others clipped by the plough, or even ploughed out by farmers given government subsidies to reclaim downland. Forestry development has damaged others.

Beyond Newbarn the road plunges down a short steep hill to

the crossroads which used to be the industrial heart of Calbourne. A hundred years ago the Sun Inn was a thatched cottage on the south side of the road, drawing its water from a well in the field behind. It was burned down in 1894 and the present brick pub built in its place, while the road now runs south of it, the line of the old one being just discernible as a narrow field.

Opposite the pub, where the garage now stands, was the timber yard, carpenter's shop, blacksmith and wheelwright's where wagons were made for farms all over the island. The timber was hauled from Swainston estate to the saw pit, hewn into planks and left to season for several years in drying sheds. (There was competition for the best trees from buyers sent out to choose timber for lifeboats to be built at Cowes: one buyer said the best ash trees in Britain grew in High Wood, above Ashengrove Farm.) The village boys would go up to the saw-pits on Saturdays and help work the two-handed band saws.

The sides and bottom boards were usually elm, ash being used for shafts, ribs and joists: wheels called for the greatest craftsmanship, each rim being made up of six sections, then bound with iron. Above the blacksmith's was the paint shop where the paint was mixed, mostly blue and red, with a little yellow, a gloss being achieved with coats of varnish. When finished a typical wagon would need five cart horses to draw it up and down the island hills.

In *The Silence of Dean Maitland* there is an exact description of a wagon made at this very yard. "Its hind wheels were as high as Alma's head. High over them arched the wagon's ledge in a grand sweep, descending in a boat like curve to the smaller front wheels, whence it rose again, ending high over the wheeler's haunches, like the prow of some old ship over the sea. A massive thing of solid timber it was, with blue wheels and red body. On the front was painted 'Richard Long, Malbourne. 1860'."

There was great competition to send the smartest possible wagon team into Newport for the Tuesday market: the carters looked after their horses with great pride and affection. One Calbourne carter reckoned his boss was stingy with oats for feed. The granary was perched up on staddle-stones so he crawled underneath, cut a small hole in the floor boards, filled a bucket with the corn that trickled through and bunged the hole with a cork ready for another day—this was common village practice on the island.

About a hundred years ago, a ploughman was working his team over a field behind the church: glancing behind to check the straightness of the furrow, he discovered the plough had turned up a whole row of brandy casks! These he hastily recovered with soil, marking each with a very small stick. This man was not a smuggler, simply one of the village—and the whole village, like Chale, Niton and Brighstone was in the smuggling trade, otherwise it could not have proved so successful. It is surprising to connect an inland village like Calbourne with smuggling: in fact it was on the direct "export route". Cargoes brought ashore along the south-west coast were brought up to the Moortown end of Brighstone at the foot of the downs. Another night's work would be to carry the barrels over the downs to Calbourne, Newbridge and eventually to Newtown from where they would be shipped across the Solent.

Today Calbourne spreads southwards from the crossroads up towards the downs, a beautiful unspoilt village, open and sunny yet sheltered by the downs, with old cottages winding round the rising green with the church atop and its other manor house, Westover, set in more parkland to the south across a picturesque stone bridge, its elegant white front shining through the trees.

The manor of Westover, or Calbourne, is mentioned as early as Edward the Confessor's reign but the present house dates from the eighteenth century when the estate was bought by the Reverend Leonard Troughear who had married the daughter of the Rector of Calbourne: later he inherited land in West Wight and acquired a barony, becoming Lord Holmes. Westover was three times inherited by daughters, whose husbands subsequently took the name of Holmes, thus keeping the family name until 1913. For a time it belonged to the Moulton Barretts, relatives of the poet Elizabeth Barrett Browning.

The present house was originally built as a hunting-lodge and behind it stands a fine range of stables and coach houses in warm red brick, ranged round a vast yard. Another drive further south once led up to the house: a broken line of huge old lime trees was evidently once an avenue, though now Jacob's sheep graze beneath them: this part of the lane was once known as Blue Doors, presumably after the entrance gates. A butler's flat was built on to the north end of the house in 1913: it was desirable to have a responsible member of the staff living in with the family silver.

The most stared at part of Calbourne is Winkle Street, a row of picturesque cottages built along by the stream, originally for Westover tenants, the oldest being those near the road, faced with chalk. For a short time, when the Barringtons of Swainston owned most of the village, it was called Barrington Row, but reverted to the old name, which means a cul-de-sac. Opposite the cottages the Caul Bourne trickles along through the stone walls of the old sheep dip, its banks bright with marsh marigolds in spring, and later with red spotted mimulus, but is not just a pretty stream, it once provided the power for five mills before falling into the creek at Shalfleet.

The first of these was a fulling mill, below Winkle Street. Today the flank of downs facing Calbourne is largely covered with forestry plantations, but once the chalk turf pastured vast flocks of sheep. After the fleece had been spun and woven into cloth, it was sent to the mill, soaked in tanks of water and fuller's earth and beaten, to shrink and dress it. Only a few banks remain: Fullingmills Farm is built on the site of the original mill.

The stream runs beneath the Freshwater road and is at once impounded to work Upper Calbourne Mill, first mentioned in 1299 when it would have ground wheat, oats and barley for the tenants of Calbourne (Westover). A deed on show in the mill records its sale in 1697 by Sir John Dillington of Knighton for sixty pounds to William Crannidge of Calbourne. In 1894 a roller plant was installed which continued to grind until 1955.

Today the mill is open to the public with its complex machinery in working order; the oldest part dating from 1664 can still be set in motion by its twenty-foot diameter water wheel. The mill ponds have been stocked with ducks and ornamental waterfowl, the banks laid out as grass walks: small weirs, footbridges and seats all add to these lovely grounds, perhaps at their best at daffodil time.

A hundred years ago there was plenty of employment in Calbourne with the two big estates, the wagon works, the mill and various farms: there were also two other blacksmith's shops, two cobbler's and more general shops than now, one at Witchingberry and another at Laurel Cottage which included in its stock "Botanical chemistry". Swainston employed a staff of eight gardeners to look after the grounds: the lawns around Tennyson's cedar were mowed by horse-drawn mowers, the horse wearing leather boots so that he should not mark the turf.

Another aspect of country life were the great shoots held on the estates: shooting is still popular in rural Wight, mainly for pheasant but on nothing like the Victorian scale. Preparations for the great shoot held for the visit of Prince Henry of Battenburg in January 1895 took almost a year. In February 1894 the keepers began their annual vermin drive, trapping stoats in drain-pipes and watching for weasels which used mole runs as their highways, as well as foxes, badgers and surprisingly even hedgehogs. The head keeper's diary reads, "Twas time for the pheasants to hatch. I heard the old hen bird fluttering and I found a hedgehog. He had forced her off the chicks and he had eaten eight and had the ninth in his mouth—he was chewing the front part while the hind part of the poor little chick was sticking out the side of his mouth." Of course danger fell from the air also in the shape of sparrow-hawk, kestrel, merlin and owls: the diary records an amazing rescue. "A sparrow-hawk came over like a flash and picked up a chick. I fired and brought it down—the little innocent chick fell with it. It was still breathing so I held it softly until it stood on its feet, then I put it back to the mother, none the worse." In April the copses were combed for nests and all the first clutches taken away to be reared under hens: there were eighty coops of these, while the wild birds would lay a second clutch and rear the chicks themselves. When the young birds were old enough to take to tree roosts, hurricane lamps were hung from trees to keep foxes away. Partridges were reared as well and by September the coverts well stocked. Not a shot was fired till the following January so that the Prince should have good sport!

The diary was kept by an island man who left school at the age of eleven in 1881 and shows surprisingly little use of the old dialect, so it must have been dying out even then. On a cottage opposite the pump is a plaque commemorating the birth of W. H. Long in 1839 whose invaluable dictionary at least preserves a written record. It is called *The Dictionary of Isle of Wight Dialect with the Christmas Boys, Hooam Harvest and Songs sung by the Peasantry*. The Christmas Boys is an island variant of a folk drama performed in various parts of England at one time and thought to be as old as the Crusades since the cast includes a Turkish Knight. It begins, though, with the entry of Great Head and Blunder.

Here comes I—Gurt Head and Blunder
If I beant a fool eddent that a wonder. . . .

The play was regularly performed every Christmas at Carisbrooke till the 1950s.

What gives the dictionary its great value and charm is the editor's habit of inserting local anecdotes to illustrate the meanings of words, for example, to snoach (snuffle): "I zay you, d'ye mind that 'ere Smith? A used to hay a miserable snoach wi'en and lived at Caaburn Bottom. One day a zays, 'What be ye gwyne to make o' your bwoy, meyaster?'

"Well, mooast likely I shall make a buttcher on 'en.'

" 'You'd better putt'n wi' wold Doctor Clarke, vor he's the biggest butcher I ever zid'!"

(Calbourne Bottom is the wooded lane that leads from the village up towards the downs and Brighstone.)

The pump stands under a picturesque conical roof of red tiles, recently restored. From it a path leads up across the hillock that makes a wide green space in the centre of the village, to the church. Since the north-west of the island is fairly flat, even this small climb is rewarded with a view right across the Solent to Sway Tower near Lymington and deep into the New Forest.

All Saints', a small church of weathered grey stone, at one time resembled Shorwell and Brighstone in having a short spire, but this was removed at the end of the nineteenth century. Its foundation is one of the oldest on the island—a grant of land was made by King Egbert in A.D. 826, though little remains earlier than the thirteenth century. It was originally cruciform but the south transept has been enlarged giving the interior an unusual squarish shape. Traditionally the north transept, rebuilt in the nineteenth century, was used by the Swainston families, and their memorials cover the walls, while the south was for Westover.

At one time an altar tomb stood in the south aisle, bearing a slightly smaller than life size brass figure of a slim youth in chain mail—this is now set into the wall while the marble columns now form part of the pulpit—for this was a false tomb. In 1383 the Earl of Salisbury accidentally killed his own son, William Montacute, in a jousting tournament: the distraught father afterwards had memorials erected in every place where he owned land—there are said to be twelve other Montacute "tombs".

Victorian restoration is responsible for the handsome stone carving of da Vinci's *Last Supper* behind the altar—and also for the shiny tiled panels beside it. The patterns of bright pink, turquoise and yellow look more suitable for a conservatory floor and are kept tactfully covered with madonna blue curtains!

In 1683 the tower was badly damaged, probably by lightning and not repaired for a long time: outside on the west face a carved inscription reads, "I am risen from ye ruins of near 70 years."

Though dozens of coaches stop in summer to afford their passengers five minutes to view Winkle Street, Calbourne remains an unspoilt farming village with roots deep in the past and a strong corporate spirit responsible for up-to-date amenities such as playing fields, hard tennis courts and a purpose-built community centre, the heart of village social life.

Several new enterprises can be found on the outskirts—a small factory turning out farm machinery is tucked behind Newbarn Farm. At Chessel Farm an eighteenth-century barn has been turned into a pottery: begun five years ago it now has a staff of twelve. Visitors can watch the evolution of a pot—and Chessel pottery is highly individual, made of porcelain and ornamented *inside* with delicate shapes inspired by coral reef and rock pool. Some is sold locally, but the major part is exported round the world, to countries as far apart as Iceland and Japan.

The latest development, down the lane to Shalfleet, is an exhibition of Classic Cars. Here one can watch old wrecks being restored to their former elegance and also visit the craft shop, which stocks only *objets d'art* made on the island.

Footpaths lead across the Swainston estate, up on to Brighstone Down, along the Caul Bourne, across the meadows to Shalfleet or over Westover Down to a different country, the wild south-western coast.

9

More Downland Villages

Miles of crumbling, amber-brown cliffs along a wild shore facing every sou'westerly gale, broken only by stream-carved chines, and above one such rugged cleft, a line of cottages along a track to the cliff edge—this is the seaward end of Brooke, while in contrast the northern end shelters under the down among huge old trees.

One hundred and twenty million years ago, before the chalk was laid down, all this land and the sea beyond was a vast tract of marsh crossed by a slow-flowing river and its streams: in the damp sub-tropical air flourished horse-tails and tree ferns, and among them lumbered the dinosaurs, from hypsilophodon, a mere five feet long, to iguanodon, the giant lizard, thirty feet long and eighteen feet high. At this time the purple clays known as Wealden marls were laid down. This stratum outcrops along the cliffs of the south-west coast and here at Brooke many exciting finds of fossil bones have been made, dinosaur bones being so commonly picked up they were often to be found around the village used as doorstops or rockery stones. In 1972, William Blows dug out a large part of a female iguanodon skeleton fron the reef below Hanover Point, described in his book *Reptiles on the Rocks* published in 1978.

The same reef embeds rafts of fossilized forest: chunks of black fossilwood spangled with pyrites can always be found along the beach. A small concrete sea-mark tower stands on the rocks, beloved of cormorants.

On the summit of the downs above stands a fine cluster of Bronze Age burial mounds, five bowl barrows, one bell, and one disc: this last has a ditch round it and another bank encircling that, but the earliest inhabitants of Brooke in historical times were probably fishermen living out on the cliffs below, now called Brooke Green. Soon after the Domesday survey the manor came into the Glamorgan family and thence to the Bowermans, who retained it for four hundred years.

In their manor house, Henry VII was entertained by Dame Joanna Bowerman, who made the king so comfortable that on leaving he presented her with his hunting horn and decreed that she was to be presented each year with a fat deer from the Park at Carisbrooke. Towards the end of the eighteenth century the ancient house was pulled down, and a new one, of austere Georgian style, erected in its place by William Bowerman. So for hundreds of years Brooke was a farming community with the Big House at its centre, and the outlying group of fishermen's cottages.

The chief catches, outside the mackerel season, were prawns and lobsters: the making of lobster pots was a flourishing industry with pots being sent as far afield as Ireland. Marshy land to the east of the village was ideal for the growing of willows—or withies as they are called locally. The pliable shoots were cut in January each year and stacked in large sheds. Later they were trimmed to size, the ends sharpened, then they were woven into the cunningly shaped baskets from which no lobster could exit.

The same wetlands provided rushes for lighting: the leaf was stripped down to its backbone, then dipped in wax. The villagers had the right to cut gorse—or fuzz, as it was called—on the common, a slope of the down.

As in most villages there was a carpenter's shop, and a busy smithy stood near what is now Downton Farm. By the nineteenth century a carrier service did form a link with Newport, but a shopping trip took all day: when a row of coastguard cottages was built west of the village, this was a major extension of the small community.

But the greatest changes were to come to the village with the advent of the Seely family who bought Brooke House, the old manor, in 1854. Charles Seely was M.P. for Lincoln. It was his son, Sir Charles, who became such a benefactor to the district, building a school at the nearby hamlet of Hulverstone, endowing reading rooms and the first free libraries on the island, while his farm-lands stretched from Brighstone to Freshwater.

At Brooke House an army of gardeners looked after the vinery and Orchard House, vast stretches of lawn and formal flower beds, a lake and water gardens along the stream. Sir Charles was greatly interested in the campaigns which eventually united a divided land into the kingdom of Italy and invited Garibaldi to stay at Brooke House, part of which was afterwards christened the Garibaldi Wing. He planted an Italian oak tree in the grounds.

A later generation entertained Queen Mary every year, when she was staying on the royal yacht for Cowes Week. One particularly fine August, tea was laid in the gardens, the butler and a bevy of housemaids spending hours laying out the best china and silver, setting up tables and chairs, arranging flowers and cushions. The Queen expressed herself delighted and was about to sit down when one wasp zoomed past her ear. "We will take tea inside," she said . . . Queen Mary also planted several trees in the grounds.

Sir Charles loved the downs, using a pony for the steeper climbs as he grew older, then in his eighties conceiving the idea of a house on the downs. So Brooke Hill was built and still dominates the west flank of Westover Down, indeed the Germans had it marked on their invasion maps as a fort! Later it was the home of J. B. Priestley, the author.

Sir Charles's son Jack Seely became a famous soldier, politician and author. *My Horse Warrior* describes how he taught his famous mount to take to the water on Brooke beach: in spite of becoming a Member of Parliament, a general and later being created Lord Mottistone, he took a keen interest in the village, and was coxswain of the lifeboat. But after he went to live in Mottistone

Manor, in the next hamlet, Brooke House and gardens fell into decay. Eventually it was turned into flats, and houses were built over the grounds, though many of the fine old trees remain.

A walk through Brooke might well begin out on the edge of the low fox-coloured cliff where stands the lifeboat house. It might seem odd at first that its double doors face inland, but the prevailing wind is the sou'west, straight off the sea, and in the teeth of a gale it would be impossible to open seaward-facing doors. The first lifeboat to be kept here was the *Dauntless*, so christened by Mrs Seely in 1860. When the maroon went up, the work of the village would stop: the rector would halt a sermon and pronounce a quick blessing since at one time five of the crew were in the church choir. The next sound was the drumming of hooves as the cart horses from Dunsbury, Brook and Hulverstone Farms hurtled down through the village. It took six of them to drag the heavy boat down to the shore and out into the sea, but ten, and all the village lending shoulders, to heave her back up the cliff after a rescue.

Many boats were wrecked on Brooke Ledge, that same reef so rich in fossils: at low tide one can walk out to the remains of such a wreck, round the point at Compton, but often the ship in distress was miles away, off the Needles or foundered on Atherfield Ledge, necessitating a long row through wild and treacherous seas. The Brooke boats saved 263 lives over their years of service: the last, *Susan Ashley*, was withdrawn in 1936, her place being taken by a fast boat kept at anchor in Yarmouth Harbour.

A path across the Green leads inland to cross the Military Road, in 1981 the cause of a revolution in the quiet life of Brooke. The road skirts the cliffs from Chale right along the south-west coast to Freshwater Bay, providing dramatic and beautiful coastal scenery beloved of visitor and resident alike: on clear mornings the far cliffs of Dorset gleam white in the sun: inland the long line of downs sweeps ever closer to the sea until, beyond Brooke, they plunge in precipitous white walls to the shore, squeezing the road between steep hillside and cliff edge. In 1981 the edge began to crack and the road beyond Brooke was closed.

This meant that all the Military Road traffic had to be diverted inland through the village itself, which led to great local indignation. Now the County Council has reopened the Military Road after having set up sophisticated electronic devices to warn of any further movement below it. Above, the slope is so steep it would cost millions to construct a new road further inland, beside eating into the downland, but it seems only a question of time before closure becomes inevitable.

Inland, the first building on the left is Hanover House, now a picturesque restaurant partly stone tiled, at one time the dairy of Brooke Farm. When workmen started to remove a modern fireplace in 1971, they found behind it an Elizabethan one, eight feet across, surmounted by foot-square oak beams which suggested it was once a large and important house, perhaps the Bowermans' original manor?

A narrow green on the right and cottages with pretty gardens lead on up towards the down, past the Seely Hall. Here every August the island Natural History Society mounts an exhibition about our countryside called Local Look. In conjunction it publishes a nature trail leaflet; the route leads up on to the downs with their characteristic chalk flora of carline thistle and rock rose, scabious and eyebright, then back through sunken lanes hung with ferns, crossing the greensand with its contrasting flora and looping back to the village across typical farmlands, Friesians out to pasture, crops of oats and barley.

As the road climbs, houses on the left disappear behind a high stone wall. This is the boundary of Brooke House and, together with the overhanging trees, hides all the new building. Presently even that is left behind, the road grows steeper, houses drop away and the village seems left behind, but no, perched up here on a hillock of its own, stands the church. The original building was destroyed in a great fire in 1862. Charles Seely then offered to give a piece of land in the centre of the village for a new church, but at a meeting of all the inhabitants it was unanimously decided to rebuild on the old site—the new church cost two thousand pounds.

The original church was probably founded by the Maskerel family, lords of Brooke in the thirteenth century, with a north chapel added by the Bowermans, and a tower built over the porch, built from a parish rate to hang one bell. A choir gallery constructed out of wreck timber from the beach was, tradition says, the origin of the fire. Afterwards much of the old stone was used to wall the churchyard, new stone being quarried close by.

The Lord of the Manor could snooze through service in his

curtained box pew: this now forms the vestry. The ornate carved pulpit of stone and marble, and the unusual trefoil-shaped marble font, both Bowerman memorials, are in complete contrast to the unplastered walls of rough stone. A small water-colour, painted before the building of Brooke Hill and the planting of its grounds, shows the church against a bare line of downs, instead of bowered in trees as now. One of the most interesting features is the lifeboat boards, rescued from the old lifeboat house and set up on the east wall, linking the two ends of the village. Here are commendations on spectacular rescues and a long impressive list of all the wrecks attended and lives saved, including the *Eider*, when the Atherfield, Brighstone and Brooke boats together saved ninety lives and the mail, and the barque *Cassandra* from which the Brooke boat alone saved forty-one.

In spring the church knoll is bright with little wild daffodils, while in summer Brooke Shute is overhung with rhododendrons.

The road eastward to Brighstone lies close under the downs largely clothed with forestry woods; and leads first to Hulverstone, only a hamlet yet important to Brooke in the past as the school was there. Though that has long been closed, Hulverstone still possesses a pub, the only one in the neighbourhood.

Mottistone, further along, is no larger than Hulverstone, but has a manor house and church. Mottistone is mentioned in the Domesday survey and later belonged to the Cheke family for three hundred years. In 1544 Sir John Cheke was appointed a tutor to Prince Edward, and after his pupil's accession as Edward VI rewarded with high office including that of Privy Councillor. But on the king's early death he intrigued with the supporters of Lady Jane Grey and was subsequently sent to the Tower by Queen Mary. A later Cheke was described by the Oglanders as "Thomas, a lewde son of a discrete father, sowlde Motson to Mr Dillington"—the family who owned Knighton.

Today Mottistone appears the archetype of an unchanged English village, the L-shaped grey stone manor beneath the hanging woods facing a green planted with walnut trees beside the small ancient church, yet this century has seen a great deal of change.

Some time in the eighteenth century a huge landslide took place behind the manor, blocking in the eastern wing right up to the roof: the rubble was not removed till 1926; when the walls came to light after some two hundred years they were found to be still in good repair. Until this time, when it was bought by the Seelys, the manor house was a farm: today the front sweep of lawn is picturesquely broken by low stone walls which are in fact the remains of the barns and farmyard. The western barn was retained and a new, imposing entrance made through it. The house, containing some modern painted wall hangings, and furniture carved by a local craftsman from cedar wood once part of East Cowes Castle, is occasionally open to the public.

The churchyard of St Peter and St Paul* can be entered on the north through a wide lych-gate with a stone coffin rest in its centre. The church was founded in the thirteenth century but much restored and altered at various times. The north chapel, originally the Cheke chantry, was refurbished in memory of General Jack Seely, first Lord Mottistone. The east windows of modern design depict angels in stained glass flying across diamonds of clear glass, whilst one tiny window presents St Peter and St Paul in more traditional jewel colours.

Opposite the church, a favourite walk leads up through the woods, and eastwards to Brighstone. Red campion, a haze of bluebells, pale bracken fronds just uncurling, larks overhead, fox and badger in deep earths burrowed in the soft Upper Greensand—this is Row Down in spring. To the north rises the steep chalk slopes of Brighstone Down where Bronze Age inhabitants buried their dead in round barrows. On Row Down only kestrels hunt by day, but once Neolithic man roamed the slopes, leaving behind stone knives and a flint axe.

To the south lies Brighstone village, part huddled round the church, part strung along half a mile of road, part large new housing estate; beyond fields, farms, a broken line of cliffs and the sea. A deep sunken lane hung with ferns, haunt of wrens and little owls, leads down to the village: local tradition says it was worn so deep by the hooves of mammoths coming down to drink and while there is no direct evidence of this, even older creatures did live here: recently the huge footprint of a megalosaurus was excavated from the shore.

The ancient grey stone church dominates one end of the street, with stone, thatch, rambler roses and pretty tea gardens grouped about it, hiding the new development. Willses, a fine example of a traditional island cottage, long and low with thick stone walls beneath deep thatch, boasts also the oldest building material. Its Queen Anne porch is built of small, thin Roman bricks, perhaps from the villa at Buddle Hole, under the downs.

This was first excavated in 1840. Its idyllic situation, sheltered from the north, open to the south and close by a spring, is similar to the Brading villa, but may have been its downfall: evidence suggests it was destroyed by a surprise attack from the north since one room was full of human bones and charred timbers. It was re-excavated in 1974 and found to be of the corridor type.

For hundreds of years the village was called Brixton: the oldest spelling is Briccheston, perhaps derived from Ecbrightston, but there was no manor of Brighstone in the Domesday survey: the oldest settlement was at Limerstone, half a mile east. The Tichborne family founded a priory there "to have a priest forever to synge for the soule of the said Nicholas of all Chrysten souls", but in the fourteenth-century the three chaplains were excommunicated for ill conduct. When Henry VIII's commissioner visited this Chapel of the Holy Spirit in 1547 it was found there had been no service for twenty years and William Tichborne had pocketed the church income. A stone table in Brighstone church is said to be the altar of the priory chapel: a farmhouse now stands on the site incorporating some of the old stones.

One of the farm labourers at Limerstone issued a petition in 1823. "Edward Downer had in his possession one quart bottle of spiritous liquors which was given him by a friend to make merry at his wedding. But a warrant was obtained and I summonsed to Newport and fined £12.10s which it is impossible for me to pay as I have no money being only a poor labourer at seven shillings per week. Therefore the smallest sum will be most thankfully acknowledged." And the fine was paid in full by sympathetic friends, many of them members of the vast smuggling fraternity of that time.

Lilygrove, a large eighteenth-century stone and tile house at the west end of the village, is said to mark the site of Uggaton Manor mentioned in the eleventh century. When James Long, carpenter, lived there he took "a harvest month", that is all the daylight hours in August, to make a vast cider press which was used by all the village. The next owner, William Russell, spread a rumour that Moortown Lane was haunted by a flying hare—so he could move his contraband in peace! A well in the garden, and the stream bed were two of his hiding places. One of the maids would put a keg in a wheelbarrow, cover it with washing and trundle it down to the Sun Inn at Hulverstone.

A pleasant half-hour walk begins by the church gate. After the French raid of 1545, Sir Richard Worsley, Captain of the Wight, ordered every parish to provide a gun. The remains of the gun house can still be seen on the north wall of the church tower. The lane leads down to a ford and bridge and the picturesque old farm of Waytescourt, thatched and stone mullioned amid green water meadows. But once a much grander mansion stood here, belonging to the Wayte family who owned most of the village from the thirteenth-century till the 1680s when Sir John Oglander of Nunwell wrote, "Wayght of Wayghts Coort hath been a very antient gentleman in our island. I bought it of him for my nephew Kempe for £2,500, so Wayght is now extinct." Old deeds show that tenants on the north side of the village could graze cattle on Row Down, and those on the south at Marsh Green Common, on the cliffs: they could also collect "fuzz" or gorse for fuel, though only what could be carried on the back, together with plough, fire and gate wood from the copses. The steward held a court at the manor when rents were paid, hence the name.

The holdings of three or four acres were usually called by the tenant's name: you can still trace these about the village. Willses for example, Mitchells, Gilmans. The rent, a few shillings a year, was sometimes paid in kind, poultry or beeswax: at Christmas "two fat capons" must be presented, and help given at haymaking and harvest.

A turn right, passing Marsh Green, brings one to the mill, still in use. A path through the gate leads along by the millpond, always full of mallard and bright with daffodils in spring, past Sheat, its terraced lawns facing a waterfall. Sheat was originally a grange of Quarr Abbey, the barns being further south on the cliffs, hence the name Grange Chine. The present house dates from 1730: beside it the trout lake was made only three years ago. Alders overhang the stream while northwards there are wide views of the downs.

The Whitsun Fair used to be a riotous time. Wagons would come out from Newport, pedlars sold fruit, nuts, gingerbread, entertainers set up sideshows and a great deal was drunk. Into this scene once wandered a young army officer and when he left he was followed and murdered here by Sheat Farm. In the early eighteenth-century there was a barracks on the cliffs, against French invasion. When news of the murder reached it, the troops marched up to the village with loaded muskets, in bloodthirsty mood, but the owner of Waytes Court interceded and they did not open fire. Of course the "Brisoners" maintained the murderer was no native, but had come "over down".

Following the road north brings one back to the church, the old graveyard beautiful with crocus and daffodils in spring. To see the interior in its full glory one must go to a service at one of the festivals to see it lit from end to end with candles in round brass chandeliers. The original church was much smaller with more of the rounded Norman arches, still to be seen on the north side. When the Limerstone chapel fell out of use, the church was enlarged to include a Limerstone chapel: later a Wayte tore that down and built a new east end, still known as the Waytescourt Chapel, while the north side was enlarged and much of the stained glass added in Victorian times. Charlotte Yonge, author of *The Dove in the Eagle's Nest,* who often stayed at the Rectory, gave the two carved chairs in the sanctuary. There is a fine fourteenth-century piscina and a fifteenth-century font, while a memorial tablet records the three bishops.

Saintly Thomas Ken composed "New every morning is the love" and "Glory to thee my God this night" while pacing the vicarage garden. On leaving Brighstone, he was made Bishop of Winchester, where he refused to entertain Nell Gwynne. Samuel Wilberforce, the church reformer, was rector for ten years, often entertaining his famous father William, who put down the slave trade. The church hall and a road on the new estate are named after Samuel, who was later made Bishop of Winchester, and a path along the top of Row Down is called Wilberforce's Walk. Doctor Moberley was headmaster of Winchester College before changing career to become Rector of Brighstone, then Bishop of Salisbury.

A church guild, called the Brotherhood of St John, once owned pasture for cattle and sheep and a church house on the site of the churchyard: these were seized by Edward VI's Church Commissioners together with two bells and a red velvet cope. The church registers reveal this together with many glimpses of national history. In 1568, church property included three sheaves of arrows: in 1625 new wheels were provided for the parish gun: by 1626 musket balls cost 1/8d: during Cromwell's Commonwealth the Rector was ejected from the parish "with insult and violence": in 1740 a bell was cast in honour of Admiral Vernon's victory.

It is nearly a mile to the shore, yet when the sea is rough the roar of it fills all the air, just as its influence has permeated Brighstone history. For example, in the churchyard stand memorials to brave Moses Munt and Thomas Cotton.

The first lifeboat to be stationed at Brighstone, the first on the Isle of Wight in fact, was the *Rescue* given by the Royal Victoria Yacht Club in 1860. By 1888 a larger vessel, called the *Worcester Cadet*, was on station in the clifftop house, coxswain Moses Munt. On 9th March the fully rigged ship *Syrenia* struck the reef at Atherfield Ledge. The lifeboat was immediately launched, but the *Syrenia*'s captain would allow only his wife and children to be rescued as he determined to refloat the ship at high tide. However, when a gale blew up, he fired distress rockets and the lifeboat struggled back to her through heavy seas. The captain was ready with a new three and a half inch hawser to make them fast, but just as it had been secured a great wave struck and it snapped like a piece of string. After a second attempt the lifeboat began to take off the crew though one minute they were deep in a trough and the next swept above the *Syrenia*'s decks. With thirteen of the crew aboard the *Worcester* cast off, but was at once overwhelmed by huge seas and capsized. Moses Munt was drowned and Tom Cotton the assistant cox, with one of the crew. Even after this disaster the boat made a third journey to rescue the rest of the *Syrenia*'s crew.

The lifeboat was removed in 1915 when a steam one was stationed at Totland Bay. Now the nearest is at Yarmouth though Freshwater Bay has a fast inshore boat.

Just along the street from the church is the pub, originally The New Inn, but recently rechristened The Three Bishops. This used to be a stop for the coach and four en route from Shanklin to Freshwater Bay, its arrival announced by a long horn blast: fresh horses were kept at Casses Farm further along. In fact history is all around you here in the village street—look for The Old Smithy and The Old Bakehouse. Some of the original field names such as

Dorrets, Greens Butt and Blanchards have been re-used as house names.

Here too you may still hear the older inhabitants using sharp-flavoured dialect phrases for which there is no real translation: "I upped and giv'un a fair ol' whistersniff"—a slap. "I'm pridner clemmed with traipsin' about Nippert"—cold through from shopping. "I'll larrup 'en one if e don't stop jackass'en about"—smack him if he doesn't stop fooling. "Tried to show'en but he got the whole boylen lot praper harled up"—all in a muddle.

Few visitors to the church ever find the little Methodist Chapel at the west end of the village, yet it has an interesting history. A group calling themselves Bible Christians began to worship together in 1831: persecuted by the community, they met in Moortown Lane—recent building revives the name Chapel Butt. Driven even from here, they were forced to meet in a chalk pit half-way up the down where they would hold services even in deep snow, until the chapel was built in 1836.

Brighstone today has a large proportion of retired people, provides a dormitory for Newport, is still surrounded by farm lands and much visited by tourists in summer, while the new estates bring in a younger element. Perhaps because of this mix, it is another self-contained village with a strong sense of community. With a butcher, grocer's, garden shop and dispensary, there is no need to shop elsewhere. You can play tennis, badminton, study sculpture, join a choir, a French circle, enjoy both disco and barn dance without leaving the village. The Spring Festival draws on local talent for exhibitions and concerts. Island Societies as a whole often have the advantage of retired professionals to pass on expertise. The school and library bring in people from Brooke and Shorwell.

An old footpath, The Packway, has recently been restored so that one can walk to the coast through fields. On the cliffs stand two holiday camps, one of them self-catering, a camp site for tents and a caravan site, yet the views are so wide, the scenery on so vast a scale that the sites make little impact on the wildness of this coast.

Grange Chine, a wooded valley, leads down to the shore. On this green shelf, the caravan site in summer, stood the lifeboat house later used as a café, though it has long since fallen to the shore and disappeared, for the tawny brown cliffs are constantly worn away, by waves beneath and water from above. But the very first flowers of spring survive, coltsfoot making gold mats over the bare clay as early as February. The paths usually disappear in winter rains and frost, but the scramble down reveals a beautiful bay, bounded by tall white cliffs of Freshwater to the west, acres of sand, black-capped gulls out on the reef, a passing oyster-catcher. Even in high summer one need walk only a few hundred yards to leave the crowds behind.

There used to be a thriving mackerel fishery along this coast, but today there are only a few marker buoys bobbing about over lobster pots. Even in 1894 the Rector was lamenting, "There are fewer fishermen than there were and I hardly ever get any fish caught with draw nets on the shore, as I used to." So fishermen, smugglers, wrecks and gallant lifeboat men have left little mark: waves thunder out on the reef and Brighstone Bay remains a lovely, untamed stretch of coast.

Eastward along the road to Shorwell, Yafford Mill has recently been opened to the public. The old wooden machinery and mill wheel are still in place, while the millpond has become home to several breeds of duck and a pair of seals, rescued as deserted pups from the North Sea. Jacob sheep and other rare domestic breeds roam the paddock, beside an adventure playground.

The finest way to approach Shorwell, though, is along the ridge of the downs from Brighstone, with views from Hengistbury Head in Dorset to St Catherine's Point: the village lies sheltered in a deep wooded bowl below in contrast to bare windswept Brighstone.

From this ridge walk, Shorwell Shute leads steeply down under a rustic footbridge through the woods—especially lovely in autumn when the chestnuts are the first to turn yellow and amber—to the centre of the village where stone and thatched cottages cluster round the church up on its mound and the old whitewashed pub, where three roads meet and each one leads to a fine manor house.

The oldest version of the name is Sorewelle, from scora, a steep rock, and wielle, a spring. In the eleventh century, the King held Shorwell. Domesday says: "Three theyns had three mansion, two villeins [tenant farmers] eight borderers [small holders] and six serfs." The overlordship came into the hands of the Redvers family until Amicia Redvers gave it to Lacock Abbey, where her daughter was a nun. The village was then counted as part of Carisbrooke parish, four miles away. This led to great difficulties, so that in Edward III's reign the people petitioned for Shorwell to be made a separate parish. One reason given was "ye greate inconvenience they suffered in carrying of corpses to be buried to Carisbrooke, through ye waltorises lanes at winter, wherebye many caught their deaths. So that ye death in winter tyme of one, caused many more."

The village was then divided into North and South Shorwell, with the Carisbrooke to Brighstone road the division between, though it by no means ran east to west: by this reckoning the church was in South Shorwell. The Abbess of Lacock provided five soldiers from the village for the West Medina Militia and employed a bailiff who leased out property which was often sublet. One such property in North Shorwell was let at the rent of one rose to be paid annually on St John's Day (midsummer). In 1529 the manor was leased to Thomas Temse for sixteen pounds a year. After Henry VIII dissolved the abbeys, Shorwell of course reverted to the king, who sold it (including Larden Copp and Slocan Copp) to Temse for just over three hundred pounds, whence it came into the Leigh family who began to build the mansion of Northcourt in 1615.

A little later the village was rocked by scandal! Sir John Oglander wrote: "George King of Shorwell and his wife, she being complained unto us by most of her neighbours that she was a turbulent woman, spoke ill of the justices, kept an ale house without licence and suspected a bawdy house and sued many of her poor neighbours. I sent a warrant." Whatever Mistress King's morals, she was evidently a woman of spirit, for she sued Sir John in the Court of Star Chamber for threatening her. Not surprisingly, this was dismissed, and Sir John concludes with satisfaction, "We were acquitted with much honour and King and his quean ordered to be whipped."

Northcourt, a tall many-gabled mansion, lies close under the downs in a hollow of the woods, hidden from the village street by thick trees. Here flourished the Leigh family, Barnabas having fifteen children. A guest wrote, "I remember not that I was ever at greater entertainment on the island, especially it being in Lent, yet there were all sorts of fish and flesh in abundance."

By the eighteenth century the owner was Richard Bull, famous in his time for his great collection of prints—some two hundred and fifty volumes, but it was his daughter Elizabeth who left her mark in stone. When her sister Catherine died she had a stone cairn erected on the downs where Catherine was said to watch the Channel waters for her true love's ship. This was known as Miss Bull's Folly, and more recently as The Thimble. When it began to fall down, the stone was carted away to make hard standing in a Brighstone farmyard, though the field is still called Monument Ground.

Elizabeth also designed a fancy dairy with coloured windows, laid out the grounds and had built for her sister a mausoleum and a memorial summer house.

By the mid nineteenth-century Northcourt was suffering from neglect. "Now become a comparative wilderness but most lovely in its desolation, charming in its very loneliness and blooming with a thousand graces amidst decay," says a contemporary guide book. It was rescued by the Gordon family, Mary Gordon being Swinburne's cousin, who took a great interest in the village, building a school with stone and timber from the estate and reclaiming Northcourt with an army of gardeners.

During the last war the house was occupied by troops. On a June night in 1941 a guard was enjoying the stillness of the summer night when he heard a bell ringing. Everyone had long been warned that church bells would be rung only as a warning of imminent invasion by the Germans. The guard commander called out the guard and rang Brigade Headquarters at Newport for instructions. H.Q. knew nothing about an invasion. When the vicar was contacted he said mildly that on still nights one could often hear the bell buoy marking the dangerous reef of Atherfield Ledge . . .

Part of Northcourt grounds are now a public space. A vast green amphitheatre above the gardens, lined with ivy and overarched with trees, is the meeting place of several footpaths—there is a map on a stand to help in planning routes, and under the mantling of ivy and garlic can be traced the shapes of Elizabeth Bull's fanciful little buildings. The rustic bridge has recently been renewed by village effort so that one can walk from one part of the woods to another high above the main road.

Along the road to Brighstone stands Westcourt Manor, presenting an L shape of mellow grey stone across a sweep of lawn, largely Elizabethan in date and belonging at one time to the powerful de Lisle family. Picturesque Westcourt is no intimidating mansion—it wears a homely air, with a farmyard beside it. Few villages can offer a more interesting walk than Shorwell, where a signpost beside Westcourt points to Wolverton, from one manor to another.

This is only a short distance but at all seasons requires boots, for it leads down into a marshy copse called Troopers through which flows a stream. Under the hazels, lush water plants mantle oozing black mud, with horsetails and willow-herbs, fragrant meadowsweet locally called cherrypie, and tiny golden saxifrage, iris and kingcups in their season, a pretty wood with a dark legend. A soldier on horseback set out to ride this short distance. He left Westcourt, rode down into the trees—and was never seen again, hence the name. Do bones of horse and soldier really lie beneath the primrose leaves?

Very soon the path emerges from this jungle right beside Wolverton Manor, built by John Dingley, Deputy Governor of the island in Queen Elizabeth's reign for £800, though an older house once stood to the north, built by the de Wolvertons, and moated round. Wolverton is the traditional E shape with a fine two-storeyed porch said to have come from the older house: the southern half had been modernized in the eighteenth century and lost its Tudor windows, while the north wing was never finished inside—an upper floor broke off into space when the Dingleys ran out of money.

By the vast stone fireplace in the great hall hang two portraits, a man and a woman dressed in the period of Queen Anne, thought to be connected with the Morgan family who once owned Wolverton, a lady, and her sweetheart killed in battle: but there is a strong likeness between the two. The pictures have been handed down with the house since they bear a curse—this will fall upon he who moves them from Wolverton. Both have been slashed (and restored) as if someone were trying to break the curse.

Long ago when minstrels were the fashion, a fiddler was employed to entertain the guests at supper and afterwards, rewarded with a purse of money and allowed to sleep in the unfinished wing. But the servants crept up on him, stabbed him to death and took the money, since when he can be heard roaming the long passages on windy nights, playing his fiddle and kicking aside the rugs.

Like Westover, the manor is the centre of a working farm, for many years famous for its Dorset Horn flock, with a fine shearing barn and granary close by.

Southwards, a maze of lanes leads through peaceful farmlands to the hamlet of Atherfield and the cliffs. The lanes leading back to the village pass by new housing, but development is on a much smaller scale than at Brighstone. When the foundations of one of these bungalows was being dug, a Mesolithic workshop was discovered, yielding hundreds of flint knives and flakes. Nearby at the village hall, Shorwell Drama Club produces plays ranging from Shaw to pantomime.

The most photographed part of the village must be the curving row of thatched cottages at the foot of the shute. These were built in 1789 for workers on the Northcourt estate: no one would guess now that several were derelict and condemned by the 1940s. Loving restoration has made this a corner of olde-world charm: in front a small patch of grass, The Green, used to be the site of the parish pump. A nearby cottage was the Northcourt bailiff's office, and the next, a pub called The Five Bells, which was closed in 1918.

Today the only pub is The Crown, parts of it sixteenth century, low-beamed and cosy, with a delightful water garden where customers can stroll between tall lilies and over little bridges. The stream which rises in neighbouring Northcourt flows on down through Troopers to Yafford Mill.

Farriers Way was named in 1970 since two blacksmiths' shops once stood along it. Above the junction with the main street and its one shop, stands St Peter's, its small tower heightened by a slender spire.

One's first impression is of delicate stonework—and that here are three churches in one, for like many island churches St Peter's has grown sideways. The church was originally a manorial chapel for Northcourt, built in about 1100, then about a hundred years later, this was rebuilt with an aisle added to the south, for the South Shorwell or Westcourt estate. In the fifteenth century another aisle was added to the south, possibly for Wolverton, and the tower added. Today the three chapels, each with a separate altar, are divided by arcades of slender pillars. Everywhere are reminders of Northcourt and its owners down the years.

John Leigh he built a great house
For this his lovely wife.
They lived at gracious Northcourt
A sweet contented life
And while he was a building
The knight said to his squire,
We'll beautify the church too
With windows and with spire.

The memorial to Sir John shows him in effigy, kneeling (on very short legs) with the little figure of his great grandson behind him, the child having died in the same week.

Many church records bear the sad words "All traces of wall paintings have now disappeared", so that those few still preserved, like the Lily Cross at Godshill, are doubly precious. Shorwell's treasure is the wall painting of St Christopher, dated about 1440, restored with great care. On either bank of a river are depicted small scenes from the life of St Christopher, but the picture is dominated by the huge voluminous figure of the saint himself, wading across with a tiny figure of Christ perched on one shoulder. The details are fascinating and wonderfully clear. The saint's feet disturb shoals of fish of several varieties: in the distance a ship is signalling to the shore: high on the bank a priest figure waits outside a hermitage reminiscent of St Catherine's Down.

Though the village obviously grew up as a farming community round its three great houses it would seem at one time to have had a fishing industry, though the coast is miles distant, for on old maps the area is patterned with withy beds, grown for crab and lobster pots. These included Haslett Withy Bed, Violets, Cranmoor's, Common Mead, and Broad Willow Bed. Today the only industry, well tucked away, is the works of Island Cottages, which makes artificial stone blocks for local builders.

All the manors are family houses: there are no tea gardens or tourist attractions nearer than Yafford, so Shorwell has remained a quiet, relatively unspoilt village. Lanes and paths wander off over and under the downs or southward through the hamlets of

Yafford and Atherfield to the sea, and though there is some through traffic, often the loudest noise in Shorwell is the cawing of rooks in the Northcourt woods.

10

The North-West Plain

Let us return for a moment to the porch of Calbourne church: from there north-west Wight undulates away in green folds to the five fingers of Newtown creek and the Solent beyond, a gentle, unspoilt land of deep, primrose-banked lanes, bluebell copses, vast fields and small villages.

Newbridge stands on a steep hillside, a pleasant mix of old thatch and newer cottages, along a winding road leading up from the Caul Bourne and its bridge which gives the village its name, though it was called Newbryge six hundred years ago. The first cottage by the stream, of handsome stone and thatch, called Normans, is thought to have been a mill house, for above it could be traced the dry outline of a pond said to serve a paper mill, but the hollow has now been used as a rubbish tip and grassed over.

A lane to the right of the bridge leads to Lower Calbourne Mill* which incorporated a bakery and brew-house. After being empty for a period, it is now a flourishing mill and bakery once again.

The village was once famous for its plum orchards, drawing buyers from all over West Wight: a hundred years ago greengages were sold for two pounds a ton. But there was industry also, quarries where limestone outcrops through the predominant clay, a brickworks with a tall chimney-stack north of the village, while at the top of the hill stood the smithy, and carpenter's shop.

When one of the cottages was repaired recently, workmen found a deep round cavity, just the size to hide a barrel of smuggled brandy, under one of the kitchen flagstones—how difficult the excise officer's job must have been. How many other island cottages had loose flagstones? But early in the last century, Newbridge had a bad reputation for swilling gin, rather than brandy. Gin could be bought at every cottage from the "vile inhabitants". Perhaps because of this, and the lack of a church, the nonconformists did their best to take over the village. In 1836 a Bible Christian chapel was built, and twenty years later, one for the Primitive Methodists, while the Salvation Army held frequent rallies in their own hall.

By the 1870s, Newbridge was a flourishing, largely agricultural community with a variety of shops, including several dairies, a forage dealer, a workshop making agricultural machinery and a variety of grocers: these included grocer and pork butcher, grocer and coal dealer, grocer and bootmaker, and, most intriguing, "John Warne, tailor and draper etc., agent for Cassell's teas, coffees and homoeopathic cocoa. Agent for Wesleyan general life insurance."

Though services were held in the village, by the end of the nineteenth century the vicar was writing that Good Friday behaviour, while improved, was still a disgrace.

One night a woman walking home through the lanes west of the village, came to a fork and turning the corner came suddenly upon a great pole upreared and the body of a man swinging from it, hanged by the neck: when she screamed, it vanished. So there grew up a tradition that a gibbet had stood here, perhaps as a warning to the seemingly lawless villagers. The name of the house nearby, Dodpits, is said to be derived from dead pits—where the victims of the gibbet were buried.

When the Freshwater to Newport railway was built in 1889, it passed north of the village, the station being in the hamlet of

Ningwood: even so this was a great step forward from the carrier's cart. The railway had a special siding to the brickworks and was also a goods line bringing coal. It was closed in 1953.

A walk through the village reveals many clues to the past: Quarry Cottage and Quarry Lane, Brickfields Lane, Clay Lane and Station Road. The Bible Christian chapel later used by the Methodists is now closed, but the Primitive Methodists' has found new life as the village hall. An attractive stone building at the top of the hill with diamond-paned lancets and a bell turret was originally the infant school and now houses a village club. One supermarket has taken the place of all the grocers, though it does not sell homoeopathic cocoa.

Since there are no cafés, antique shops or even a car park, Newbridge seems untouched by tourism and that large sign The Orchards brings to mind the plum season. But no, The Orchards is a holiday centre, with caravans, chalets and a heated swimming pool, so tucked away it is invisible from the village. The chapels must have had some effect—there is no pub at all now!

While Newbridge did not grow from a medieval manor, nor has it a church, Shalfleet, to the north, is the complete feudal English village, church, manor house and pub grouped closely together, with a mill and quay to the north. The flat road from Newport takes a sudden dip at the head of a creek and here the village has grown up, dominated by the church on its rise. The name began in the ninth century as Scealdanfleot, meaning a shallow stream, though in fact the creek is not visible from the village street.

After the Normans, the manor came into the hands of the Trenchard family, for some three hundred years, Walleran Trenchard having left his name on the south part of the village, now called Warlands. Henry Trenchard was excommunicated for besieging Titchfield Abbey, and later was accused of poaching deer from the King's Forest of Parkhurst, and mowing down and carrying away the King's crops at La Panne (near Newport). Later it belonged to the Worsleys of Appuldurcombe, then merged with the Swainston estate.

The flat lands around Newtown creek had always been vulnerable to invasion, so that when the church tower was built, it was surely conceived as a refuge, if not a defensive position. A church stood here before the Normans, but it was they who raised this extraordinary tower unlike any other on the island, squat and massive as a fort, walls five feet thick at its base and only to be entered through the church. Its unchurchlike appearance has evidently been a worry down the ages, for eighteenth-century drawings show it capped with an incongruous cupola, a little dome pointed at the top.

Then, "Shalfleet poor and simple people/Sold their bells to build a steeple" as the old rhyme says. The dome was removed and a wooden steeple erected in its place: this in its turn became unsafe: older residents remember it being pulled down in 1912, so that now the tower, though re-footed and much buttressed and repaired, stands as the Normans built it nine hundred years ago.

The people were not actually as simple as the rhyme makes out, for the bells were never rung *in* the steeple, only in the tower below and the church, judging by its accounts, seems never to have been without bells. It seems probable that they did sell two bells to the neighbouring church of Thorley, where a medieval bell is engraved with the name Walleran Trenchard.

Inside, the church is dark at the west end, where a great arch leads into the tower. In one corner lie two ancient raised grave slabs, one bearing traces of a shield and spear: the reredos was made from an Elizabethan communion table: above the north door an enigmatic carving seems to represent a figure, possibly Daniel or Mark, standing with each hand on the head of a lion. The church lost the name of its dedication at some time in its long history, and was dedicated to St Michael the Archangel only in 1964. Though little remains of the Norman nave, the interior of the church escaped the Victorian craze for tiles and retains a stone-flagged floor beneath rough stone walls: some of the Victorian box pews remain at the back, their walls almost shoulder high, though the wooden choir gallery has gone.

The stained-glass window which is a war memorial holds two surprises: in one panel stands a conventional St Nicholas in flowing robes against a conventional sunset and palm tree, but look closely and the silhouette of a submarine can be seen against the sun: similarly a small biplane zooms through the clouds above the head of St George.

Just below the church, a cottage with a picturesque roof line, now a private dwelling, was once the clergy house. Opposite, well back from the road, Shalfleet Manor's oldest walls are Elizabethan. On the corner of Mill Lane stands the New Inn and across from it an old stone house at one time called Malthouse, where the beer is said to have been brewed. Behind the church lies an estate of new bungalows but this is tucked away from the old village. Its chief quarrel with the present is the traffic which streams through the village street, particularly in summer, since this is the main road from Newport to the ferry terminal at Yarmouth: the local residents continue to campaign for a bypass.

The working heart of the village used to lie down the narrow lane past the pub. Here, before falling into the creek, the Caul Bourne turned one more mill, valued in Domesday at eleven-pence. Working in conjunction with the bakery opposite, the mill supplied much of West Wight with bread and flour deliveries until the 1920s: one of its great wheels was brought from the derelict Kents Mill at Carisbrooke. Today it is a private house, painted pink—a footbridge leads past it and through a little oak copse towards Newtown.

The main track leads through a gate to Shalfleet Quay, five minutes' amble with fields on the left and a grassy bank falling away into the creek on the right, beginning as a narrow channel with a fringe of woodland along the further bank, slowly widening out to join the main creek. A pair of swans glide past with three cygnets behind them, a godwit in smart black and white probes about the tide line with his long beak, and a solitary curlew flies overhead. A few small boats lie at anchor or pulled up on the bank.

The quay itself juts out into deep water. Its sea walls made of boulders are said to date from the seventeenth century. Winter and summer there's always someone messing about with a boat, turning over the engine, painting: in summer quite a crowd of boats anchor around the quay: it is a favourite visiting place with the New Inn just up the lane, locals run dogs and people come from other parts of the island to picnic. But even in high summer the quay is not commercially busy as it was in the last century and even earlier when it was port for the Swainston estate.

Picture a great warehouse and stores behind the quay, boats coming in from the mainland loaded with coal and sometimes slate, unloading on to lines of waiting wagons, then loading up with corn for the return journey: while beyond the quay gangs of men worked the salterns. Further down the creek stood a brickworks, with a house for the manager—at one time John Lindsey, whose descendants emigrated to America, one of them to become a famous mayor of New York.

Today two small sheds huddle against stone gable ends, which are all that remain of the warehouse, while a few humps betray the broken banks of a salt pan. All traces of the brickworks vanished when the creek was used for invasion practice during the last war. Now Shalfleet Quay and most of Newtown repose in the arms of the National Trust, safe for yachtsmen, walkers and the crying gulls.

The brickworks stood on the western bank, divided from the quay by another arm of the creek, Western Haven, and reached by a lane further west, leading to Hamstead, even today remote from the main road and a far cry from Regent Street in London. For that very reason it was chosen by John Nash, the famous architect. In 1798 he married Mary Ann Bradley and in the same year began to build himself a pseudo-Gothic castle at East Cowes. Close friendship with the Prince Regent brought him many royal commissions such as the Regent's Park terraces, while his island connection brought him work on a smaller scale. In 1813 the Corporation of Newport passed a vote of thanks to him "for the very elegant and masterly plans for the construction of the new Town Hall, which in the most liberal and flattering manner he presented to the Corporation".

Previously in 1804 he had bought an old house at Hamstead, renovated it as a shooting box and installed his wife there with her large adopted family of infant cousins by name of Pennethorne. He did not spend much time there himself, and in his will left none of his wealth to the Pennethorne tribe. Local people felt that selfless Mrs Nash was rather hard done by. But Shalfleet is a long way from court. There it was said that pretty Mary Anne had been the Prince Regent's mistress, that Nash married her to oblige his royal friend, and it was further rumoured that some of the adopted children were not Pennethornes at all . . . All legal papers pertaining to them were destroyed by the Duke of Wellington. Perhaps Hamstead once harboured a royal family then, of a kind. John Pennethorne grew up to be a well-known architect in his own right.

Nash described himself as a "thick, squat dwarf", but was

obviously a man of outgoing charm and kindness. Though seldom there, he took a deep and benevolent interest in the Hamstead estate, building the brickworks and donating land to provide work for the poor of Shalfleet.

Ningwood Manor also lies within the parish, its estate reaching back to Domesday. Richard de Redvers, Governor of Wight, gave it to the Priory of Christchurch at Twyneham. His successor, Isabella de Fortibus, gave the convent permission to enclose the land with dykes and hedges, "save that the doe with her fawn should have free passage". At the Dissolution, Ningwood was given to the Hopson family. A later Hopson, John, was captain of the local volunteers and friend of John Milton—they had neighbouring town houses in London. The poet, whose own wife had left him in 1642, wrote a sonnet to Lady Margaret Lee, Hopson's wife, and "this lady, a woman of great wit, had a particular honour for him and took much delight in his company".

When John Nash bought this eighteenth-century house, it lay opposite Ningwood Green, with its blacksmith's shop and common rights for fourteen horses and seventy-five sheep—but the green has all disappeared since the building of the railway and the school. Later the manor belonged to Dr Wyndham Cottle, another local benefactor who provided almshouses and a new hospital wing, while the estate was left to the R.S.P.C.A., becoming a home for retired horses. Until recently old pit ponies, ex-police horses and pensioned off beach donkeys could be seen enjoying the peace of these green meadows, but the home has now been moved to the mainland to save the high cost of ferry charges.

Some hundred thousand years ago, between ice ages, great beasts roamed over this land—huge horned bison and elephants with six-foot tusks, but Newtown Creek first enters history with the Danish raid of 1001 when a shore settlement is said to have been burned and pillaged. The Bishop of Winchester later came to own the large estate of Swainston which included the creek and by his orders a new town was laid out on its banks with a grid of streets laid out as precisely as any twentieth-century development, Gold Street and High Street running east to west, Broad Street and Church Street crossing them at right angles: between them the land was divided into burgage plots or smallholdings. While the tenants had to pay rent, they were free of the usual

Shalfleet

Shalfleet Church

Salterns at Newtown

Newtown Creek

Remains of the old church, Thorley

The newer church, Thorley

Old Freshwater

Freshwater Bay

View from the Causeway, Freshwater

All Saints' Church, Freshwater

Potter at work, Totland

The pier, Totland

The Broadway, Totland

A greengrocer's, Totland

manorial duties and tithes, hence the name Francheville, or Freetown, the original name of Newtown on the east bank of the creek, founded in 1218.

The French raid of 1377 seems to have begun the decline of Newtown, though it had a mayor and borough charter still in 1598 and was returning two members to parliament. A scheme to reclaim part of the marsh then fell through, but about 1700 a vast area of salt flats was enclosed by a bank with two sluices to control water levels. Part of the new land was used as salterns, for Newtown despite its name had become a mere village dependent on agriculture, fishing and salt making. At about the same time, though, a new town hall was built, for Newtown continued to send two members to parliament until the Reform Bill of 1832. Albin, writing in the eighteenth century, said, "It is plain that the four members of Newport and Yarmouth are returned by only two persons. The members for Newtown are chosen at present by four persons: in all six members by six electors only." The population by this time was about seventy and the thirteenth-century church of St Mary Magdalene had fallen into ruin. During the early nineteenth century the town hall was used as a school.

The salt industry flourished, though; there were six sites altogether including that at Shalfleet Quay and another on the eastern peninsula. The three largest would share a load of coal brought in by ship. A saltern consisted of several rectangular ponds, divided from the sea by high banks and filled with sea water a few inches deep: as the sun evaporated the water, what was left became strong brine. At Newtown this was drained off along a ditch into a pit near the brick boiling house, from which it was pumped up to the boiler—the pump was a hollow tree trunk with a wooden piston. Boiling crystallized the salt which was then sent off from the jetty by boat. It was the opening of the vast Cheshire salt mines which destroyed the island industry: the Newtown salterns closed down early this century.

Later one of the salterns was used to breed oysters from spat, but conditions were wrong and the infant shellfish died. Nearby an attempt was made to grow asparagus, but this too died out. But over on the eastern entrance to the creek, yet another brick-field flourished, and all through the nineteenth century a certain amount of river trade was carried on. Captain Holbrook, for example, sailed the *Wellington* to and fro from Dorset with cargoes of Portland stone for island builders.

At the end of the last century the village had a resident colony of coastguards, a pub, several dairies and Woolgar's grocer's shop. The pub, properly called the Newtown Arms, became known locally as Noah's Ark, presumably because of the coat of arms above the door, depicting a leopard in a slightly ark-like boat. J. H. Woolgar, who kept the shop, wrote a little book about Newtown in the 1880s in which he says of one dwelling, nonchalantly, "The house served its time but passed into decay and collapsed. This is the fifth house that has collapsed within the last twenty or thirty years to my knowledge." He also burst into verse:

> The Town Hall stands on an eminence overlooking the harbour,
> And in the past within its walls you might hear a good palaver.

Today Newtown is a little hamlet scattered between arms of the creek, pastureland, hazel copses and salt flats, on the way to nowhere, its only large population the gulls, waders and geese out on the marsh, now protected as a nature reserve, a green and peaceful corner of the island with little traffic even in high summer and fascinating to explore on foot.

From Shalfleet the lane crosses a narrow stone bridge over an arm of the creek called Causeway Lake—to the west where it widens out stood the old quays, long disappeared, though the shapes still show up in aerial photographs. A narrow channel winds away between the mud flats, curlew crying in the distance: in winter flocks of black and white lapwing fly in, while August purples the banks with sea lavender. Not a house in sight . . . Walk on down the lane, though, and there is the Town Hall, a sturdy brick building complete with balcony for announcing election results and open to the public in summer: the wide grassy space on which it stands was part of Broad Street.

Just beyond lies one of the few old stone houses in Newtown, once the village pub, with the coat of arms still above its door. Here the tarmac lane turns to the left into High Street, but look to the right also and there is the eastern end of High Street continuing as a wide grass path.

The Reserve's reception centre has recently been moved here into the middle of the village and a visit to it enriches any visit to the marsh itself. There are check lists of birds, displays of waders and gulls, a chart showing how the marsh develops its wealth of vegetation, maps and photographs of the village, a fifteen-foot fire iron used in the brickworks and most spectacular of all, the fossils. The skull of a bison measures more than four feet from horn tip to horn tip, the tusk of a straight-tusked elephant at least six. These date from a period between ice ages, some hundred thousand years ago.

Along High Street stand a few cottages, old and new, and the village pump with a large iron wheel. This was the principal street of the town, as the name implies and it is still possible to see the lines of some of the old burgage plots on either side where gardens or hedges still divide the land into small parcels, though this was more evident before hundreds of elms were lost in the epidemic of Dutch elm disease. At Woolgar's cottage the lane swings right—it once continued straight on down to the quay.

A church was built here at the time of the founding of the new town, and dedicated to St Mary Magdalene, at whose feast an annual fair was held, but this fell into ruin: the present small building, rather chapel like, with a bell turret at the west end dates from 1835. One of its most interesting features is a horrific drawing of the old church about 1800, a roofless ruin with only three walls standing and all overgrown with trees.

The lane turns another right angle, out of Church Street into Gold Street, though the eastern length is gold only with buttercups. A footpath leads down to the marsh where the grass banks of the old salt pans still enclose shallow water where tern dive for fish, though the salt house is now only a heap of bricks.

Round about 1700 the marsh to the east was reclaimed. This must have been an enormous undertaking, involving the building of a sea wall and sluices round one hundred and twenty acres in a blunt triangle, all of which became pasture land. A map of 1768 shows it as land "Property of Sir Thomas Worsley, Bart" with salt pans at the tip. All this was changed by the great tide of 1954 which breached the wall and flooded the pasture, returning it to mud flats. Ever since the quarter mile of remaining sea wall has been a much-loved walk, but at the end of 1981, a tide as high as that of 1954 with a north-easterly gale behind it made a fresh breach, allowing the sea into the salt pans.

But on the reserve there is an interesting new development. A few years ago ten pairs of little tern used to nest out on the Brickfields peninsula, then the numbers dwindled away to nothing probably because of thoughtless picnic parties landing from boats. So it was decided to create a new and safer habitat to encourage the tern to come back. In the summer of 1980, with the help of a grant from the World Wildlife Fund, the Scrape was created. The word scrape, since it can describe the depression made by a bird for its nest, suggests some minor pond: the Scrape is in fact a wide lake with a high bank all the way round and a deep ditch outside that to keep out predators. The four islands have been prepared to provide different levels of vegetation: for example, one is gravel over polythene to encourage little tern and oyster-catchers which favour an almost bare shore.

While there is plenty of nesting space on the reserve, many nests are lost every year, swept away by spring tides: in the Scrape the water level can be controlled so it is hoped the mallard, shelduck, ringed plover and redshank will move in too. A new hide overlooks the lake.

Newtown is still invaded. Every winter huge flocks of Brent geese fly in and browse for months around the grassier reaches of the creeks, often flying right over the village, darkening the sky with their wings and filling the air with a hound-like yelping. Herons and kingfishers fish the inland channels, while copseland provides a different habitat altogether.

The oyster fishery has recently moved from the village into the centre of Town Copse, where clams and oysters undergo their final cleaning in large tanks. Never mind coals to Newcastle, clams are now being exported from Newtown to the United States! The National Trust has lately wrought a great change in the copses by reviving the traditional method of coppicing, that is harvesting hazel, ash and thorn by cutting poles near ground level and leaving the tree to sprout anew, in a ten-year cycle. The neighbouring copse, Walters, used to be treated this way and is now one of the richest in the island, botanically speaking, with one hundred and forty different species—coppicing lets in sunlight, of course, and encourages growth on the copse floor.

The poles were used largely for the making of sheep hurdles: now they are a useful part of coastal defences; made into mattresses and covered with rubble and planks, they help protect the sea wall from further encroachment by the sea.

Lanes wander off eastwards to the hamlet of Porchfield, and westwards to Shalfleet. South of that village, many of the old hedges have been grubbed out, turning the land into a cereal-growing prairie which seems out of scale in this gentle, rural landscape. Ningwood and Wellow hamlets straggle along quiet roads, merging with each other and the small village of Thorley. Though the sea is not far distant, rising land and forest cut it off from view much of the time; the low clay cliffs constantly crumble away, making access and coast walking difficult—Thorley seems an inland place.

The earliest farm of this name was Torlei, a thorny place—and it had to be kept that way. Thorley's only importance in the twelfth century was as a rabbit warren. Isabella de Fortibus, who owned the manor, granted a tithe of rabbits annually to Christchurch Priory, and it was forbidden to clear the undergrowth lest it deter the "conies" from breeding. Five hundred was reckoned to be a year's harvest. After the priory had taken their share, the rest were sold at twopence per head "for the benefit of my lord, the King".

Another theory as to the name derives it from the Norse god Thor and quotes the somewhat unreliable but picturesque *Anglo-Saxon Chronicle*. "The Danes went into Wihtland and there they roved about even as they themselves would and nothing withstood them nor any fleet by sea durst meet them—a heavy time." The Danes did raid the island in A.D. 1003 and this low-lying country from the western River Yar to the creeks of Newtown has always been vulnerable. Even during the last war, Shalfleet had a parish invasion committee with contingency plans for cooking without electricity and housing the homeless.

A little stream, Thorley Brook, runs westward, falling into the Yar estuary, of little importance but for the question of the mill. Yarmouth tide mill, just upsteam of the harbour, a solid, mellow brick building now used as a private house, would appear to be in the middle of the town, but was always claimed as part of Thorley as it stands beside the confluence of brook and river. In 1892 Yarmouth Town Trust tried to levy wharfage on corn shipped to the mill, and flour shipped from it. The tenant wrote in hurt tones, "I have to state that the mill is in the parish of Thorley, that the channel leading to it has been provided with posts by myself nearly fifty years that I have been tenant."

Pevsner describes Thorley Manor Farmhouse as "perfect William and Mary". Its crop survey for 1832 shows that this was always fertile corn land, before the destruction of hedges. There were seventy acres of oats, forty-two of barley and 135 of wheat, with six for peas and beans and a surprising number, forty, for turnips. Right beside the farmyard stood the church.

This is said to have been founded by Amicia, Countess of Devon, in the thirteenth century and, like the rabbits, was given to Christchurch. "In a wooded vale at a brief distance from Yarmouth, opening upon the placid ripple of the Yar and facing to the south the precipitous heights of Afton, embosomed within a wooded vale, all tranquil and lonely stands the quaint and ancient church of Thorley," says a guide of 1870, but this idyllic scene was about to be shattered.

The nineteenth century saw many changes in Thorley. New roads and bridges were built, a parish school opened in 1867 and though the population was only about one hundred and fifty, it was decided to build a new church. This has no tower but a striking turret for two bells over the porch. Built of stone without, the inside is curiously lined with yellow bricks, and patterned with red ones: its most interesting features concern the old church, a splendidly massive thirteenth-century font, its stone base green with lichen, the ancient bells from Shalfleet, a drawing of the old church looking rather like a farmhouse, and the churchyard walls which were built of stone from the old church.

Thorley Street joins Wellow and Thorley, a mixture of old cottages and modern houses, often with fields between. Wellow has a shop, but the Literary Institute, once the pride of the place, is now derelict. There are footpaths, but most of them are field tracks, so on the whole this is not the most interesting walking country. One of the pleasantest corners of Wellow is the lane leading to the ford and footbridge: on one side horses graze beside a cluster of old stone barns while on the other side of the stream stands Brook Cottage, once home of the novelist Margaret Campbell Barnes. When alterations were being made, she was delighted to find a smuggler's hide in the bank of Thorley Brook, and another inside the chimney. Other hides in Wellow, some in barns, prove that it was on the "export" route from Brooke to the north coast.

Thorley Manor Farm and the site of the old church used to form a picturesque corner of Thorley: recently the erection of a Dutch barn has almost obscured the old church from view, but it is worth a visit. A footpath leads across a field to the graveyard and in the middle stands a tiny building, stone with a tiled roof, its height out of all proportion to its size, massively buttressed, facing north and south. In fact this is merely the porch of the old church with its north end filled in so that it might be used as a mortuary chapel, though now it no longer plays even that humble role and sheep graze the turf around it.

The low-lying meadows behind are often flooded in winter, providing an extra habitat for gulls and swans. To the west the Thorley Brook winds down to the River Yar and beyond it rise the heights of the Isle of Freshwater.

11

The Isle of Freshwater

A pair of redshanks are courting on the frost-whitened mud flats: the male performs a little dance round his mate, on long orange legs, then they rub beaks together: a rowing boat at anchor scarcely moves in the sluggish stream: up above the west bank the old grey church stands among a few cottages—here on the causeway over the Yar, in winter, it is still possible to imagine the village of Freshwater. (For today its red bricks sprawl almost from one coast to the other and it has all the shops you expect in a town.)

This western peninsula of the island is all but cut off from the rest by the Western Yar which rises only yards from the Channel and flows out on the north into the Solent. For hundreds of years this causeway was the only link, for though the Yar itself is here narrow, it has wide tracts of marsh on either side. On old maps the whole area is named Isle of Freshwater and as late as 1638 plans were drawn up to breach the pebble bank at the Bay and replace the causeway by a drawbridge. "The parish of Freshwater by a cut overland between sea and haven may easily be made an island fit to receive the people of the country, their cattle and supplies from the main island, in case of invasion."

The line of the causeway was once a mill dam, with the mill buildings in the centre: as the total fall of the Yar, from source to mouth is only about twenty feet, it is thought this must have been a tide mill, like the one lower down at Yarmouth: the ruins disappeared when the causeway was widened. Another great change was the coming of the railway, extended from Yarmouth. The line ran right along the east bank of the Yar: today the old track makes a pleasant walk into Yarmouth, or southwards into Freshwater where a garden centre occupies the old platform—the support walls are still visible from the footpath.

The peninsula was originally divided into King's Freshwater, Prior's Freshwater and Weston, the ancient communities being called after compass points, Norton, Sutton, Easton, Weston, and Middleton. Norton Green survives as a hamlet on its own, Sutton has become Freshwater Bay, the other names being still in use: Weston Manor is now in Totland, a new village formed out of Freshwater.

In 1635 then, Freshwater was a parish of scattered farms with a nucleus of cottages on the river bank by the church. That year the curate, John Hooke, had a son Robert. Though partly crippled and soon left an orphan, Robert found a patron who sent him to Oxford where he began his career as a scientific inventor, later to become the great innovator of the seventeenth-century, responsible for many mechanisms now taken for granted, including the watch spring. So it is entirely fitting that the hill leading down from the church should be named after him, and that the factory built at its foot, on the site of the old station buildings should be Acorn Springs.

By 1800 the scattered population of the parish numbered only about six hundred. By the middle of the century France had recovered from the Napoleonic Wars and began to build iron-clad warships. This was taken as a direct threat of invasion and so a major fort-building programme was begun to protect The Needles Channel route to Portsmouth. Freshwater Redoubt, overlooking the bay, was built in 1857, followed by Needles Battery and Fort Warden on the north coast, 1863, Hatherwood

Point Battery opposite the Needles above Alum Bay, 1865 (also large forts in the Yarmouth area), all of which brought new trade to Freshwater. Brickworks opened up and the village spread westwards. Some officers built their own houses in the area.

It is difficult to imagine the enormous impact of the railway. Until then an expedition to Newport by wagon or trap, thirty miles there and back was a major undertaking involving an early start, nursing the horse up and down steep hills, taking five or six hours on the total journeys—and Newport was not only the market town and centre of trade, but the place where you picked up the news of the rest of the island and indeed the national news. Of course it was the commercial impact which was of greatest importance and Freshwater continued to grow.

The fashion for seaside holidays, Queen Victoria's love of the island, and the fame of the Tennysons at Farringford combined to draw visitors to the sheltered northern beaches and so a new kind of development began and a whole new area of building sprang up to cope with the holiday trade. By 1900 the population had increased to more than four and a half thousand. Rival horse buses competed for trade outside the station to take visitors to the coast, north or south.

By this time School Green was a shopping and trading road as it is now; there were the Assembly Rooms, the Royal Standard Hotel, a large nursery, a hardware and furniture shop called Dowty's, an engineering works and a smithy, often with a queue of horses waiting to be shod so that the street always smelled of burning hoof—the horses were of great benefit to the nursery who employed local boys to bring in handcarts of dung.

But in 1906 a devastating fire broke out destroying much of this scene. Dowty's was a three-storeyed building packed with cartridges, paint and drums of oil and the only fire engine was a manual pump brought by troops from Golden Hill Fort near Yarmouth, totally inadequate to fight such a blaze. Shortly after, a similar fire destroyed the hotel, so that the present shops and Royal Standard with its elegant porch are the result of the rebuilding.

There were two other blacksmiths, and brickyards had sprung up all round. Small one-man yards operated at Copse Lane and Afton, larger ones at Totland and Meaders in what is now Tennyson Road, where a man was paid six shillings for each thousand bricks made by hand by slapping clay into an iron mould.

Shingle for the building trade was dredged from a bank in the west Solent and brought in a flat-bottomed barge called *Frederick* to the beach at Colwell, where it was run aground at half tide. When the tide had ebbed, carts were drawn out by horses and loaded up with baskets of shingle, extra trace horses being called in to drag the heavy load up the chine and the whole operation had to be timed to finish before the tide came in.

Wood was also in demand. At the carpenter's shop in Tennyson Road a man would work a fifty-six hour week, finishing at four o'clock on Saturdays. For rough work, sawing timber out of tree trunks, he would get fourpence halfpenny an hour, for skilled carpentry, sixpence. As well as all the housebuilding, this shop made two bathing machines which were manhandled down to the beach when finished and drawn up under the cliff each evening by windlass.

The various forts, still manned, continued to have an impact on Freshwater. The local volunteers also used the forts for practice and had their own military band in navy blue uniform. Many officers were quartered in the village and it was a common sight to see soldiers marching through the streets. This ditty was sung in the pubs during the Boer War.

One two three—the Boers are after me!
Four five six—they chased me with their sticks.
Seven eight nine—they missed me every time.
Hard times in the Boer camp tonight!

Pubs which have since disappeared include the New Inn at Norton, and the Spin Fish: turn-out time could be a pretty raucous hour.

Other kinds of entertainment included visits from Baker's Fair, complete with elephants and a steam organ, and a travelling theatre performing melodramas such as *The Rake's Progress*, and *Murder in the Red Barn*. The sweetshops sold acid drops, bull's-eyes, peppermints and cough lozenges, together with local delicacies called Ukumsnivvy, and wibblepupes. A deep muddy ditch draining down to the marsh was a favourite place for larking about.

Today that ditch is a stream running through the mown grass

of School Green, especially pretty when hundreds of daffodils are in bloom or the chestnut trees in flower. The long street includes shops of every kind now from supermarket to fashion boutique: the latest amenity, achieved entirely by local effort, is a covered swimming pool.

Having traced the rise of Freshwater one is better able to understand the history of the old church on its river bank. All Saints' was one of the six island churches mentioned in Domesday and given by William Fitz Osborn to the abbey of Lyra in Normandy. This was a very small church on the site of the present south aisle and the only remains of it is a carved archway now moved into the north porch. As the village grew so did the church, the most dramatic addition being the tower which was built up through the existing western end and has a tall, striking archway pierced right through to provide a west window. By the latter part of the nineteenth century even wooden galleries built over the north and south aisles could not accommodate the influx of parishioners and a major expansion took place in 1875, giving the church three gables instead of one. This was done with great care so that today one would think the whole building to be ancient. Inside, it is spacious and full of interest, the walls of rough cream and brown stone since the Victorians stripped off the plaster.

Memorials bring to mind the various manors which originally made up the parish, not all of them within the Isle of Freshwater. The north aisle was originally the Compton Chapel: on its wall is inlaid a fine small brass depicting Adam de Compton in armour, while in the south aisle, originally the Afton Chapel, are two bare matrices, once brasses of the Lords of Afton: even with the brass missing the black silhouettes form a fine memorial.

The chimes of the tower clock, added in 1895, were specially composed by Sir John Stainer and called "The Tennyson chimes" since this is the church used by the Tennysons—their names are all about, with memorial tablets to Lord Alfred, "whose happiest days were spent at Farringford", to Lady Emily his wife and to their sons, while a statue of St John commemorates Lionel, who died at sea aged thirty-one. A curious stained-glass window reproduces a painting by George Frederick Watts, who came to live nearby, depicting one of the King Arthur stories made popular by Tennyson's poems, the angel appearing to Sir

Galahad. The angel's face is Lady Tennyson's while the Knight is Ellen Terry, the actress.

Another unusual feature, not often found in churches, is a large-scale map of the parish for 1839. This shows the whole area divided up into small parcels of ground, some of them like Headon Common Field still farmed on the strip system, some smallholdings, all with their proper names such as Great and Little Zilcombs, Cow Ground, Rough Borough and Fluetts. It is also possible to trace individual features—Windmill Field to the south-west where a windmill stood as early as the twelfth century, Sheepwash Lane near to it, and out on the far point, a circle marks the first Needles Lighthouse, which was built on the top of the cliff.

The view from the churchyard stretches from the downs on the south to the forest of masts in Yarmouth Harbour: at high tide the Yar spreads out like a lake below the walls, since today sluices under the bridge prevent it flooding Crundell Marsh above: in spring the turf is brightened by thousands of crocus and while ancient yews and beeches remain, dozens of young trees have been planted to take the place of the elms lost in the epidemic of Dutch elm disease.

The spread of Freshwater occasioned the building of a new church at Norton Green: St Andrew's was built in fourteenth-century style, but congregations rise and fall: today St Andrew's is closed and lies sadly neglected, awaiting secular development.

In 1894 the western area was made into a separate parish, so Totland became a village in its own right including the hamlets of Colwell and Alum Bay. Obviously really old houses are scarce. Windmill Farm is near the site of the windmill long since disappeared: Rockstone Cottage, built in 1790 at the head of the lane leading to Colwell Chine, was the officers' mess when soldiers camped on Colwell Common during the invasion scare of the Napoleonic Wars: Sunny Cottage in Summers Lane has a strange history.

There was no need for the men of the first Needles Lighthouse to live in the lighthouse, since it was on the cliff top. Separate quarters were built close by. In the 1850s it was decided to build the present lighthouse, at sea level for better visibility. The stone was brought from quarries at Portland directly by boat and unloaded on Totland beach where it was cut to shape, numbered and inspected before being reloaded and towed out to the Needles rocks. Offcuts of the pale Portland stone can still be found on the beach. When the cliff-top crew's quarters were no longer needed, they were removed and re-erected in Summers Lane.

But the major part of Totland sprang up in the latter part of the nineteenth century, indeed many of the houses were planned by the same architect who would not allow slate to be used, so there is still a preponderance of orange tiled roofs, which on larger houses often break out into little turrets and towers. These, the mellowing of a hundred years and the growth of many trees, lend Totland its individuality today. Many of the houses were built for "overners" as summer residences, as in Seaview; paddle steamers called at the small pier bringing visitors direct from the mainland; guest houses sprang up. Totland, recently the haunt of fishermen and smugglers, had become a fashionable resort: the visitors organized an annual regatta in the bay, followed by fireworks. Locals competed to meet passengers off the pier with hard-luck stories worthy of an Irish jarvy.

"Cab, sir? Got a wife and six children to support, sir. I play the organ down Colwell Chapel, sir, regular."

Such a surge of building created a huge demand for bricks. The largest brickworks grew up in The Avenue, the road joining Freshwater to Totland. Here stood a large kiln with a tall chimney that was a local landmark for many years. Dowty's produced not only bricks but chimney pots, finials, flower pots and of course red tiles. These were sent all over the island, first of all by horse-drawn wagon, then by traction engine to Freshwater station: some were even exported to the mainland.

All the pottery items were very fragile and breakages so frequent that new roads such as The Mall were made up with damaged goods from the brickyard. Today the drying shed for tiles can still be seen in The Avenue, though now converted into an antique shop.

The forts also continued to be a source of trade, often using local contractors for building new gun emplacements. In 1901, for example, local labour built a special jetty at Colwell Bay, with concrete blocks and railway lines, for the landing of new, heavy guns for the Needles Battery. All the village turned out to see the guns inched up the beach on heavy trolleys shoved by local troops and pulled by a traction engine.

Totland and Colwell face the comparatively sheltered waters of the Solent: much of local life was connected with the sea. All through the eighteenth and nineteenth centuries small boats would leave to lay nets or pots round the Needles—and be gone for a peculiarly long time, having in fact rowed across to France and back for a more valuable catch! One elderly lady remembers her grandmother's predicament when the Customs Officer called before the last two barrels could be carted away. When he came in saying he had orders to search the whole house, she shrugged her shoulders and said he must get on with it then but not expect her to help him, she'd too much washing to do. Only when he eventually left empty-handed did she move away from the wash tub, for the barrels of spirit had been hidden under her voluminous skirts. It must have taken extraordinary skill and strength to row a boat across the Channel by night, and as in the parallel story of James Buckett* of Brighstone, both skill and strength were used also to save lives.

Though not subject to the terrible storms and rocks of the Channel coast, ships were often wrecked off Totland by running aground on the shingle bank near the Needles Channel. Money was collected from all the children in island Sunday schools to buy a lifeboat and this, called *The Little Dove*, was installed at Totland. Later in 1884 the R.N.L.I. provided the *Charles Luckhombe* and a brick lifeboat house was built above the beach with a steep slipway up which the boat was hauled by winch. One of the families most closely connected with the lifeboat, not to mention fishing trips, was the Conways. When a new lifeboat was needed, William Conway was asked by the R.N.L.I. to tour the coast of Britain inspecting lifeboats and to choose the most suitable model for Totland—he normally traded out of Yarmouth on a coaster called *Emma*.

He was unable to find a suitable boat, but took plans of the bow of one, the stern of another and so on: a new lifeboat was built on the Thames to these requirements and put on station where she remained until 1924 when her place was taken by the fast new boat at Yarmouth. The long story of brave rescues was painted up on "Lifeboat boards" and set up on the walls of the lifeboat house.

One night the maroon went up, the lifeboat set out through great waves for the shingle bank. After an arduous row into the teeth of a sou'westerly gale they found a small coaster run aground, the seas running right over her at times so she was in imminent danger of being dashed to pieces. In the howling darkness with only a pitching lantern for light, they managed to rescue the crew and had just cast off and begun the return journey when the cox heard a cry aboard the wreck. When questioned, the captain said it was only the old cat which he hadn't bothered about. Cox Conway immediately ordered the boat to return, scrambled aboard, found the distraught cat and buttoned it into the big pocket of his oilskin. None the worse, the cat lived for years as a pet of the Conway family.

With the last boat gone, the lifeboat house was used as a bathing hut: one day it was discovered the lifeboat boards were missing. Though police and locals combed the neighbourhood they could not be found: the records were by now insufficient to compile a new wreck history. Then, years later, the boards were found: they had been used to build a chicken house! A local craftsman rescued them, repaired the damage with wood from an ash oar, repainted the faded letters and now the boards are set up for all to see in the Parish Hall. Jack Conway, the only surviving member of the boat crew, saw them unveiled in 1974.

A wreck which brought thousands of sightseers happened in April 1908. During an unseasonal blizzard, the steamship *St Paul*, outward bound from Southampton, collided with the light cruiser *Gladiator* just off Norton Green, tearing a great hole at the water line level with her engine room. Amid clouds of steam and smoke the *Gladiator* keeled over only yards from the shore. Rescue attempts were hampered by a foot of snow. All through the summer, tugs attempted to salvage her. Finally, in October, huge concrete bollards were built on the shore and by the aid of a steam windlass the *Gladiator* was eventually righted and towed away to Portsmouth amid much cheering and hooting of ships' sirens.

As Totland had begun to grow, the community felt the need for a church of its own, and a wooden one was erected in Madeira Road. But of course a "posh" resort needed something grander and Christchurch was built west of the village, on the hill, a splendid example of Victorian Gothic. Today, the main door leads straight into a meeting place, carpeted with blue, ringed with easy chairs upholstered to match which gives one first a feeling of surprise and then of welcome—beyond stands the wide nave and south chapel. A massive lych-gate is carved from the timbers of H.M.S. *Thunderer* which fought at Trafalgar.

The house called Weston Manor, a home for the handicapped, was built in 1871 by the Ward family whose money was also responsible for St Saviour's Roman Catholic church, a handsome brick building, but another church building in Totland is seldom recognized.

Today Colwell Common is a pleasant open space: gipsies no longer camp there, indeed are seldom seen on the island now. The lane leads down to a gap in the low cliffs, called a chine but hardly to be compared wih the dramatic fissures of the south-west coast. Chalets and beach cafés cluster round its mouth. The newly renovated sea wall leads round to Totland Bay with its pier and sandy beach. Walk its length on a stormy day and it is easy to realize why coastal defence costs so much here. Waves break against the massive concrete slabs with a noise like thunder, sending sheets of spray high into the air, while on the landward side the low cliffs sag and slump.

Right at the western reach of the sea wall still stands the lifeboat house and its steep slipway. There are several dwelling houses and some chalets on the wall, and a large wooden hut now used as a café. In fact this is the original church of Totland, brought down here after the opening of Christchurch and at first used as a library.

A steep lane leads up to the Turf Walk along the cliff top and beyond to the main street, a smaller and more scattered shopping centre than Freshwater, though still hardly village like: interesting shops include a working pottery, and antique clock centre. Many of the ornate villas originally built as family summer residences are now guest-houses or flats. The huge turreted hotel which dominated the cliff above the pier lay derelict for a long time and has now been demolished.

It is a long time since troops marched through the streets: the redundant forts have met varied ends. Cliff End has been demolished, Fort Warden houses a holiday camp, Golden Hill has become a small industrial complex with a country park outside the walls, while Hatherwood Point Battery, up on the heather slopes of Headon Hill has largely fallen away, over the cliff. The path over Headon from Totland has lovely views across the

Solent, and south to the stark white cliffs above the Needles. At the foot of the hill a chine leads down to the famous cliffs of coloured sand on the nearer side of Alum Bay.

Twentieth-century building has joined Freshwater, Totland and Freshwater Bay in one sprawl so that it is difficult to know where the boundaries stand. Freshwater Bay is not technically a separate village, but is so different in terrain and atmosphere it must be described by itself. Old Freshwater looks across the marshes to the calm estuary of the Yar, Totland, bowered in trees, faces the sheltered Solent from its low crumbling cliffs, but Freshwater Bay, rugged and wild, ringed with great white walls of chalk and facing into every Atlantic-born gale, is another world.

A commercial directory of the island published in 1871 restricts itself largely to manorial history, church descriptions and lists of residents, but with the Freshwater Bay entry, the writer is overcome and bursts into lyrical prose: "Here lies all that is bright, beautiful and marvellous in nature; the rocky cliffs, seven hundred feet above the level of the sea, standing on whose cloudy heights one hears from afar the subdued roar of the plangent wave, like the distant murmur of a great city; the wondrous caverns all lost in gloom . . . in this sea girt nook lies the very marvel of the Divine handiwork."

For hundreds of years the small bay was deserted, too wild to sustain even a fishing hamlet. The first cottage seems to have been a solitary inn, referred to as The Cabin. In 1799 a Dr Lynn lent one of his patients his cottage in Cowes for a change of air. The patient was Ann Morland, her husband the artist George Morland, a great character always in debt through his generosity to friends and addiction to drink. Soon after their arrival in Cowes he received news from his brother in London that his creditors were about to pounce, so they left hurriedly for the remoter shore of West Wight where Morland frequented The Cabin, delighting in the company of smugglers and fishermen.

"Where else can I find such original models?" he asked, when taxed with keeping low company. He was always a great joker and one night hauled up the lobster pots in Freshwater Bay, replacing bait or lobster with various farcical "catches" including a boot, a turnip and a wig. He and his friends hid behind the rocks next morning to watch the fishermen's faces, but when they had had their fun, jumped up and paid for the lost fish.

On another farcical occasion he was taken to be a spy for the French. At the time "Look out or Boney will get you" was the local catch-phrase, invasion much feared and the natives naturally edgy. Morland was marched to Newport, accused of making plans of fortifications for the enemy—that is sketching Yarmouth Castle—and a drawing of a spaniel's head was produced in evidence as a map of the island! Once more he was rescued by his friends.

But Morland genuinely loved the wild south-west coast and worked hour after hour turning out such pictures as *Wreck of Indiaman off The Needles, Freshwater Gate, Coming Storm in the Isle of Wight, Smugglers,* and many unofficial sketches dashed off to pay for drinks. Two pubs, The Horse and Groom near Shalfleet, and the Fighting Cocks at Arreton, once sported signs done by his hand.

By the early nineteenth century a hamlet had grown up round the bay, which included two hotels, The Albion which is still there, and Lambert's Family Hotel and posting house, on the cliff above. One of the sights of the neighbourhood was Freshwater Cave, a rock cathedral one hundred and twenty feet long. "The cavern is divided into dim recesses, by massive pillars . . . rare and fantastic forms are continually being developed. This cave once enjoyed the considerable reputation as one of the chief lions of the island."

But the greatest lion of Freshwater was undoubtedly Alfred Tennyson: seldom can the arrival of one man have had such consequences for an area. In the middle of the thirteenth-century, the Prior of Domus Dei in Portsmouth, one Walter de Farringford held the lease of some land in Freshwater: his name has come down the ages to this now famous house under the downs. Alfred and his wife Emily came to look at the house one November day. "As they gazed from the drawing room window out through the distant wreath of trees towards a sea of Mediterranean blue, with rosy capes beyond, the down on the left rising above the foreground of undulating park, golden leaved elms and chestnuts, they agreed that they must, if possible, have that view to live with." So they leased it.

Three years later Emily wrote in her journal: "We have agreed to buy. Went to our withy holt: such beautiful blue hyacinths, orchises, primroses, daisies, marsh marigolds and cuckoo flowers. A thrush was singing among the nightingales and other birds mad with joy." One of their first callers was Prince Albert, dropping in from Osborne.

So this little village, the most isolated of island communities, became the literary focus of England: among the writers came Edward Lear, Lewis Carroll and Longfellow, while other visitors of divers talent included Sir Arthur Sullivan, Darwin, Ruskin and Garibaldi. Ordinary visitors flocked to Freshwater on the offhand chance of a glimpse of the poet striding through the village in his wide black hat and flowing cloak, or standing on the rustic bridge across the lane declaiming his latest poem.

The locals, glad of all the new trade, remained level-headed. "If 'e don't want folk to stare at 'un, why do 'e wear that outlandish ol' rigout?" one was heard to ask. Another local joke was the question, "What d'ye want to run then, once round Freshwater, or twice round Tennyson's hat?"

Some came on visits, others actually to build houses of their own. George Frederick Watts, the painter, lived at Holland Park with a family called Prinsep. When their lease expired he bought land next to Farringford and built a house for the Prinseps called The Briary with a large studio, so that they could all be near their friend Tennyson. (This original Briary was burned down.) Watts married Ellen Terry, the actress, when she was very young and he twenty years her senior: they spent their honeymoon at Freshwater, but the marriage was over eighteen months later. Now it can be seen why her face and Emily Tennyson's appear in Watts's church window.

Sarah Prinsep's sister Julia was to have almost as much impact on the bay community as Tennyson himself. Staying at Farringford she decided that its mild climate would benefit her husband Charles Cameron and bought two cottages which she had joined into one by a castellated tower, christening the whole Dimbola after a coffee plantation the family owned in Ceylon. Though the elder of their six children were by now grown up and gone away, the Camerons had adopted three orphaned relatives, Cyllene, Melita and Sheridan, and now acquired two more, great nieces, Mary and Adeline, as well as a servant's child, Mary Ryan.

In 1863 with Charles away inspecting the coffee plantations,

Julia Cameron felt depressed: to give her a new interest her daughter Julia presented her with a camera and dark-room equipment. By this time the locals were used to the "goings on" at Dimbola, for Mrs Cameron was a woman of driving energies, ardent friendships and impulsive gestures, determined to overfill every minute of the day so that she frequently had to pursue the last postal collector in a donkey cart with a sheaf of letters and kept the little post office busy daily sending off telegrams by the half dozen. At the age of forty-eight she channelled all this energy and enthusiasm into photography, to become the most famous photographer of her time. A chicken house was turned into a studio and the coal-house became a darkroom. Since portraits became her speciality, the household was pressed into service: Cyllene appears as Ophelia, Mary Ryan as Egeria. The Prinseps and Tennysons also appear frequently. Then the village became used to Mrs Cameron flying out of Dimbola in a red cloak and seizing any passer-by with an interesting face, who would be whisked into the studio, draped in a curtain and posed as King Arthur or the May Queen. Farringford's visitors were a rich source, including Anthony Trollope, Charles Darwin and Henry Longfellow.

Meanwhile the fishermen went on fishing, guest-houses sprang up to accommodate the less famous visitors and a new fort, Freshwater Redoubt, was built above the western curve of the bay, bringing more inhabitants. During its construction much of Freshwater Cave beneath was filled up: various other caves exist to the west, with romantic stories hinted at in their names—Lord Holmes' Parlour, for example—but these can only be reached by boat.

To make concrete blocks for Redoubt and other forts, shingle was taken by the ton from the beach at Freshwater Bay because it was readily accessible beside the road, but this was very short sighted as the shingle bank formed the only barrier between the sea and the source of the Yar in the marsh below. So concrete promenades were built—also using the shingle—partly as coastal defence, partly to provide a more civilized resort for the visitors. This was misguidedly built below the high spring-tide line and before the end of the century had already been undermined, its blocks scattered on the beach. In the winter of 1905 a southerly gale so heaped up the sea that it burst right through the sea wall and at high tide waves thundered through the breach right across the road and into the marsh.

A more permanent building dates from this time; St Agnes is the only thatched church on the island and appears with its long low profile which sinks easily into the landscape, and its weathered stonework, to be much older than it is. A stone near the entrance is carved with the date 1694—one of many brought from a ruinous seventeenth-century farmhouse at Hooke Hill.

St Agnes is a delightful church inside, all uncluttered stone and pale wood. The low window-sills and clear glass allow both a view of the cliff meadows and the sun to stream in. The east end is an apse, the beams above it radiating across the roof like a second sun: the screen beautifully carved with vines and lilies was the work of a local craftsman.

It was Lady Tennyson who chose the dedication, after Lord Alfred's poem "St Agnes Eve". Not to be outdone, Julia Cameron arranged her maid Margaret in a saintly pose and photographed her as St Agnes—a print hangs on the wall.

Today the Isle of Freshwater is securely linked to the rest of Wight by various roads and bridges, but it still retains something of an outpost atmosphere, becoming largely self-reliant for its social life and entertainment. Though a cinema has come and gone, there is a golf course on the downs with spectacular views all round, art exhibitions and the library, swimming clubs, choirs, and several flourishing dramatic societies, as well as an Arts Society which brings professional artists and musicians from the mainland.

Totland caters for a large number of holiday residents in summer, while a vast number pass through to Alum Bay, with its coloured sands, chair lift and views of the Needles. Though there is accommodation round Freshwater Bay—including Farringford which is now a hotel—many of the visitors come for the day: it is also a place much loved by island people, a favourite end to the spectacular coastal drive along the Military Road. The closure of that would inevitably mean fewer visitors, winter and summer.

The most striking view of the bay comes from the west. Walk down the road from Farringford, round a bend and suddenly there is the sea—above you, with white cliffs and three great stacks jutting out into the waves, Mermaid, Arch and Stag Rocks, beloved of gulls. The promenade keeps the sea at bay—sea wall is a better word since it is not tarted up for tourists—and leads west to a rocky beach where the chalk cliffs curve round in a white wall making Freshwater a tiny almost enclosed cove like a miniature Lulworth. One or two fishing boats may ride at anchor, a flight of herring gulls sail in with their wild cries, a pair of black cormorants fly out to their breeding ground at the Needles.

Coach drivers have been known to palm visitors off with the Freshwater stacks instead of driving out to Alum Bay and the Needles proper. One puzzled visitor asked, "If those are the Needles, where is the lighthouse?"

The driver said in shocked tones, "It's only towed out at night. You don't think they'd leave it out there all day, do you?"

Fort Redoubt still looks out from the cliff top, though now converted into a private house.

The walker can set out on two long-distance trails, the South West Coast, fifteen miles of exhilarating cliff to Niton, or the Tennyson Trail over the downs to Carisbrooke. For contrast, part of the marsh has recently been laid out with grass walks and seats, a flat circular potter with a wealth of marsh plants and birds, sheltered from the sea winds.

But the most spectacular walk on the island must be from Freshwater Bay along the western end of the Tennyson Trail,* along the ever-narrowing green crest of the 700-foot cliffs between Channel and Solent, a bird sanctuary, on the farthest tip of which lies the Needles Battery, built in 1863 to cover the sea channel up to Portsmouth. Thirty years later another was built, higher up on more stable ground and called New Needles Battery. During the last war both were in use. After the war the whole peninsula was taken over as a testing site for rocket engines, and made out of bounds to the public.

When the National Trust bought the headland in 1975, they faced an enormous task simply to make it safe, since it was littered with half-ruinous buildings, machinery, underground workshops and tunnels. Now the forts are being restored, Old Needles was opened to the public in 1981: soon it will be possible to reach even further west—a tunnel leads down to a searchlight emplacement perched right above the Needles, their chalk bastions shining white between clouds of upflung spray and eddying flocks of gull and guillemot, a fit place to leave the reader who has travelled westwards from Foreland through the infinite variety of island villages.

Index